God's Springtime

God's Springtime

Joyce Huggett

Illustrated by
Sister Elizabeth Ruth Obbard ODC

the bible reading fellowship

Text copyright © 1992 Joyce Huggett

Illustrations copyright © 1992 Sister
Elizabeth Ruth Obbard ODC

Cover illustration © 1992 Pauline Deane

Published by
The Bible Reading Fellowship
Peter's Way
Sandy Lane West
Oxford
OX4 5HG
ISBN 0 7459 2336 4

First edition 1992
Reprinted 1992 (twice)
All rights reserved

The Scripture quotations are from:
The Good News Bible (GNB) © American Bible
Society, New York 1966, 1971 and
4th edition 1976
The Jerusalem Bible (JB) © Darton, Longman &
Todd Ltd and Doubleday and Company Inc.
1966, 1967 and 1968
The Living Bible (LB) © Tyndale House
Publishers, Wheaton, Illinois 60187. 1971
The New International Version (NIV) © New York
International Bible Society 1978
The New Testament in Modern English (JBP) ©
J.B. Phillips, 1960, 1972

A catalogue record for this book is available
from the British Library

Printed and bound in Malta

Acknowledgments

I am indebted to the Abbess of West
Malling Abbey for originally allowing me
to use their picture of *The Return of the
Prodigal* in my book *Open to God*, and I
am grateful to Hodder and Stoughton for
letting me use their photograph of the
picture in this book.

I am grateful to the Presentation
Convent, Matlock, for granting me
permission to use a reproduction of their
prayer card *The breaking of bread*.

I am grateful to Tessa Spanton for
permission to use her drawing of a
blossoming thorn.

The tapes mentioned in this book are
available from the following sources:
Open to God, Hodder and Stoughton.
Laudate, Veritas Publications.
God's Springtime, Eagle.

Contents

Acknowledgments

I count it a privilege to have been invited to write this book which marks the seventieth birthday of the Bible Reading Fellowship. A whole variety of people have supported me in the writing of it and I would like to make mention of a few of them.

First, my thanks go to Shelagh Brown who initiated the invitation and who has been a most kind, thoughtful and supportive editor. Next, I would like to include Dennis Napier, former Director of BRF whose courtesy and support I appreciated while the book was in its infancy.

Next my thanks go to Father Paul, the Assistant Librarian at Mount St Bernard Abbey who directed my reading at the research phase and to Father Tony Nye who journeyed with me as I prayed through some of the material on the Passion of Christ.

I have never met Sister Elizabeth Ruth Obbard ODC but I have felt greatly supported by her partnership and prayers as we have worked together on this book, and I have gained a great deal through using some of her illustrations during my own prayer times. I have also valued the help, interest and co-operation of another artist, Pauline Deane who contributed the painting for the front cover of the book and the inlay card of the tape.

David Wavre, Managing Director of Eagle, introduced me to Pauline Deane. He has helped me in other ways including producing the tape which some individuals and groups will enjoy using alongside this book.

My husband took *God's Springtime* on retreat with him almost as soon as it was written. He used it for his own time of stillness and, as always, I am grateful to him for his shrewd comments and suggestions.

Finally, I would like to thank two other friends who have been my prayer companions in the past and whose insights I have assimilated so that they now feel like my own. One is Sister Pamela CHN, with whom I once led a Lent Retreat where we presented some of the insights contained in these pages. The second is Bishop Stephen Verney who, both in conversation and through his book *The Dance of Love*,[1] has broadened my understanding of concepts like forgiveness and repentance and who has helped me to feel awed by mysteries; to recognize that these, like God, in the words of *The Cloud of Unknowing*,[2] 'by love . . . can be caught and held, but by thinking never.'

Joyce Huggett, August 1991

For David
Friend and Fellow-traveller
With thanks

Introduction

'What is Spring?' asks the poet, Gerard Manley Hopkins.

> *Growth in everything—*
> *Flesh and fleece, fur and feather,*
> *Grass and greenworld all together ...*[3]

> *Nothing is so beautiful as spring.*[4]

Kenneth Grahame's character, the Mole, seems to agree:
'The Mole had been working very hard all the morning, spring-cleaning his little home. First with brooms, then with dusters; then on ladders and steps and chairs, with a brush and a pail of whitewash; till he had dust in his throat and eyes, and splashes of whitewash all over his black fur, and an aching back and weary arms. Spring was moving in the air above and in the earth below and around him, penetrating even his dark and lowly little house with its spirit of divine discontent and longing. It was small wonder, then, that he suddenly flung down his brush on the floor, said, 'Bother!' and 'O blow!' and also 'Hang spring-cleaning!' and bolted out of the house without even waiting to put on his coat. Something up above was calling him imperiously ... so he scraped and scratched and scrabbled and scrooged, and then he scrooged again and scrabbled and scratched and scraped, working busily with his little paws and muttering to himself, 'Up we go! Up we go!' till at last, pop! his snout came out into the sunlight, and he found himself rolling in the warm grass of a great meadow.
'This is fine!' he said to himself. 'This is better than whitewashing!' The sunshine struck hot on his fur, soft breezes caressed his heated brow ... Jumping off all his four legs at once, in the joy of living and the delight of spring without its cleaning, he pursued his way across the meadow till he reached the hedge on the further side.'[5]
And so his adventures began. Adventures which opened up new

vistas, new friendships, new pleasures, new sorrow—and much personal growth.

From the fourth century on, the Church became increasingly aware of 'the spirit of divine discontent and longing' which prompts Christians to take action during the weeks leading up to Easter. That was one reason why Lent became an important part of the Church calendar.

The word Lent comes from the Anglo-Saxon word 'Spring'. So Lent came to be known as God's Springtime; the period when Christians tuned into God's love and made a fresh response to it.

Pancake Day

These early Christians took their faith so seriously that they spent much of Lent fasting. Because they abstained from meat, eggs, and dairy produce, housewives cleared their store cupboards of such foodstuffs on the day before Ash Wednesday and made pancakes from the ingredients. Shrove Tuesday was a red-letter day for another reason. This was the day when all catachumens, or converts and enquirers, enrolled for the compulsory pre-Baptism classes. Every day during the weeks leading up to Easter, these young Christians would receive instruction in the form of Bible teaching and personal prayer ministry so that by Easter Sunday, the day of their Baptism, they would be ready to take their vows: to promise to turn to Christ and to live their lives for him. It was on Shrove Tuesday, too, that more mature Christians resolved to review their life and commitment to Christ: to embark again on the journey from winter to spring, from death to life.

While enthusiasm for pancake tossing, pancake parties and pancake races seems never to have died, interest in Lent has waxed and waned with the years. Recently, the number of people expressing a desire to take Lent seriously seems to have increased. Individuals set aside extra time to pray and reflect on certain Bible stories and small groups form for the purpose of reflecting together.

This year, I would like to suggest that, like the Mole, we heed that 'something up above' which is calling us and that we also embark on a journey—a journey into God. I propose that we start on Pancake Day, Shrove Tuesday and that we aim to reach our destination on Easter Sunday. I have made this particular journey on several occasions. Each time it has brought a spring-like renewal: new understanding and new love, new strength and new purpose, new sorrow, new repentance and new healing, new life and fresh cleansing, a new song which rises from a 'new' heart, a new vision for the future and a fresh awareness of God.

I like to make this journey during Lent but I have made it at other times also. A spiritual Spring-time can take place during any of nature's seasons, so although this book was written with Lent in mind, its contents can be used at any time of year.

Whether we set out on our journey in spring or summer, autumn or winter, it is important to be aware that the starting line is just where we are. We need to be aware, too, that there is no need to make elaborate preparations like throwing a pancake party. We come just as we are. But we do not travel alone. Our first travelling companion is the prodigal son. He shows us how to make a start.

Next we journey with Jesus, first into the wilderness, then to the Mount of Transfiguration and finally to Jerusalem and beyond.

We take the journey slowly—one step at a time, meditating on over-familiar stories in bite-size pieces. The value of this is that, just as it is those who stop and stare who see colour peeping out of early rhododendron buds and daffodils dancing in the breeze, and just as it is those who sit and listen who hear the cuckoo's call, so it is those who will stop to stare and listen to these ancient but ever-new truths who will be enriched by them and by God. To encourage the stopping and the pondering, I have used a variety of translations of the Bible. The more modern translations are not necessarily the ones I like best or would most recommend for regular reading, but their starkness sometimes pierces our complacency and forces us to sit bolt upright and pay attention.

Most people using this book will be busy people: commuters who will use the book in the train, professionals who will add this Lenten discipline to the other priorities with which they continually juggle, parents with scarcely a moment to call their own who will have to snatch precious minutes to read and reflect, the sick and the elderly with plenty of time but little energy for prayer and meditation. And others. Perhaps the unfamiliarity of some of the passages will help such people to plumb the depths of the mysteries we shall encounter as we travel.

Whoever we are, we will gain most from this book if we remember four things:

▷ pray as you can, don't try to pray as you can't

▷ set aside a regular time each day if at all possible to read the Bible verses and the comment slowly and prayerfully

▷ remember that the project is probably the most important part of the prayer time because this is your personal reflection. This reflection can take place while you pray, if you have time, or at odd moments during the day—as you walk to work, wash the dishes, change the baby's nappy, take a coffee break . . .

▷ pray the prayer, which will possibly draw from you a more personal response which rises from your own experience. And if you are using this book with a group of other people, follow carefully the suggestions made for such groups which you will find at the back of the book.

Since many of us will be setting out on this journey together, perhaps we could sometimes remember to pray for one another? The prayer I have prayed for those who will use this book is an adaptation of a prayer Paul prayed for the Christians in Ephesus: that our roots may go down deep into the soil of God's marvellous love and that we may each be able to feel and understand the breadth and length, the height and depth of that unending love. That we may be filled afresh with the fullness of God.[6] I pray, too, that by the time we reach Easter Day we may be able to echo Gerard Manley Hopkins' paean of praise:

> As sure as what is most sure,
> sure as spring primroses
> shall new-dapple next year,
> sure as tomorrow morning,
> amongst come-back-again things,
> things with a revival,
> things with a recovery,
> Thy Name.[7]

Let him Easter in us,
be a day-spring to the dimness of us . . .
Gerard Manley Hopkins,
'The Wreck of the Deutschland'

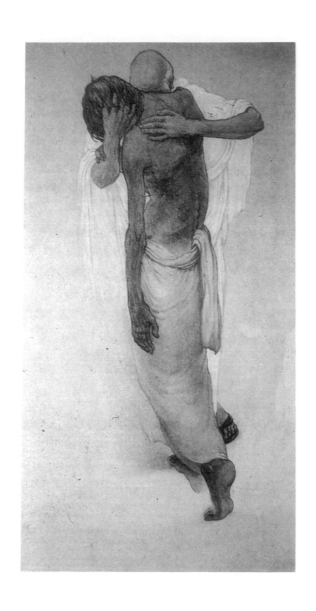

Beckoned by Love

Once there was a man who had two sons. The younger one said to his father, 'Father, give me the share of the property that will come to me.' So he divided up his property between the two of them. Before very long, the younger son collected all his belongings and went off to a foreign land, where he squandered his wealth in the wildest extravagance. And when he had run through all his money, a terrible famine arose in that country, and he began to feel the pinch. Then he went and hired himself out to one of the citizens of that country who sent him out into the fields to feed the pigs. He got to the point of longing to stuff himself with the food the pigs were eating, and not a soul gave him anything. Then he came to his senses and cried aloud, 'Why, dozens of my father's hired men have got more food than they can eat and here am I dying of hunger! I will get up and go back to my father, and I will say to him, "Father, I have done wrong in the sight of Heaven and in your eyes. I don't deserve to be called your son any more. Please take me on as one of your hired men."' So he got up and went to his father. But while he was still some distance off, his father saw him and his heart went out to him, and he ran and fell on his neck and kissed him. But his son said, 'Father, I have done wrong in the sight of Heaven and in your eyes. I don't deserve to be called your son any more . . .' 'Hurry!' called out his father to the servants, 'fetch the best clothes and put them on him! Put a ring on his finger and shoes on his feet, and get that calf we've fattened and kill it, and we will have a feast and a celebration. For this is my son—I thought he was dead, and he's alive again. I thought I had lost him, and he's found!' And they began to get the festivities going.

(Luke 15:12–24 JBP)

The Start of the Journey

One of the things I love about spring is the surge of energy which seems to pulsate through the whole of creation giving birth to a host of new beginnings: new buds appearing on bushes, new blossom bursting from cherry trees, new primroses peeping from hedgerows, new aconites and snowdrops, daffodils and bluebells popping up in gardens and meadows, new carols coming from blackbirds and thrushes, new lambs leaping on uncertain legs. The world not only looks and sounds different, it smells different. Better.

Just as, in spring, life seems to pour from the ground into every bud and blade of grass, so in the springtimes of our lives, God seems to pour new energy into us. The poet Ulrich Schaffer put it well in a prayer poem:

> *I sense your drive*
> *To flow through me*
> *Into the smallest blood vessels*
> *Because you want to be my heartblood*
> *In all the passages of my life*
> *And you want to become visible in the leaves*
> *And the fruit I bear*
>
> *Spread out in me*
> *Press forward, penetrate, pierce and flow*
> *even if, at times,*
> *I want to repeal this invitation*
> *Being afraid of your ways in me.*

Circulate in me
Change and renew
Because I know
That only your Spirit
Can bring real life and fruit.[8]

Jesus once told a story about a young man who one day experienced within himself such a resurgence of energy. The youth was one of the world's 'lost' children. He had demanded from his father the inheritance which would one day come to him, left home with it and lived as though his father was already dead. For a while he enjoyed his freedom to the full. But famine and fast-dwindling funds stopped him in his tracks. Thoughts of home and father surfaced. A sudden surge of energy turned the whisper of a suggestion into a resolve:

I will go home to my father . . .

(Luke 15:18)

Jesus told this story together with two others: the lost sheep and the lost coin, because he wanted his listeners to grasp the true nature of God: when anyone is lost, God's heart aches so much that he searches for them until they are found. When they are found, his joy knows no limits. In the words of the father in this story: 'We must celebrate with a feast.' (Luke 15:23)

A Project

Pascal once painted a beautiful pen picture of God: 'We could not seek God unless he had already found us.'[9] As you think about that claim, recognize that the fact that you are using this book suggests that God is calling you back home—giving you the desire and the energy to return to him.

A Prayer

Pray, slowly and meditatively, Ulrich Schaffer's prayer poem.

The Waiting Father

A service of Holy Communion is held in many churches on Ash Wednesday. During the service, some worshippers have the sign of the cross traced in ashes on their forehead. That is why the day is known as Ash Wednesday.

For some people, being marked with the sign of the cross in this way symbolizes their desire to do what the lost son did: to return to the Father.

Through the Ash Wednesday readings, God begs us to come back. These readings assure us that the God who calls us is 'gracious and merciful . . . full of steadfast love' (Joel 2:13). It was to show just how loving God is that Jesus told the story of the prodigal son.

Having explained how the younger son had resolved to return home, Jesus places the spotlight on the waiting father. He tells us that while the son was still a long way from home, 'the father saw . . . his son.' (Luke 15:20)

When you see something which is a long way away, it is usually because you have been scouring the landscape for it: like travellers on safari peering through binoculars for a glimpse of wildlife or like children on a day-trip to the beach competing with each other to see who first catches sight of the sea.

When you scrutinise the landscape in this way, it is almost always because you want very much what you are searching for. The father, it would seem, was searching for the first sign of his son's once-familiar figure because he was willing his son to return home.

Jesus assures us through this unforgettable story that God loves us like that. He is not an austere, aloof, unapproachable Other. His love for us is so strong that he even plants within us the longing for him which eventually reaches out for him. Then he waits patiently until we respond to his love.

A Project

Draw a picture or diagram which sums up the way you see yourself in relationship with God at the moment. Draw a second picture or diagram which sums up the way you would like your relationship with him to grow. Try not to judge yourself. Instead talk to God about your pictures.

A Prayer

Read this prayer slowly. Echo the words if you can. Or notice where you are not quite ready to pray in this way.

O Most Creative One, ever bringing me to new life
O Most Powerful One, empowering me for life's journey . . .
O Beloved One, loving me as I am,
Have you noticed that I'm coming home?
I have seen you, the All-Seeing One who sees me
I can remain away from home no longer . . .

My soul proclaims the wonder of your friendship
My spirit is weeping within me for joy
My heart spills out tears with delight
They mix with joy and I tremble
feeling totally claimed by your love.[10]

The Compassionate Father

Thomas Merton once wrote: 'The God of Ash Wednesday is like a calm sea of mercy. In him there is no anger.'[11] The father in Jesus' parable of the lost son is like that. Jesus tells us how he felt about his wayward son: 'The father's heart was full of compassion.' (Luke 15:20)

What was it that filled him with compassion? Was it the bare feet or the skeleton-like figure? Was it the gaunt face or the bedraggled body? Was it the lost youth or did he, father-like, see deeper into his son than that—to the disillusionment, the despair, the lost virginity, the dashed hopes, the humiliation, the worldly wisdom gained at such a high cost? Did he see the broken heart, feel the rejection and tune into the loneliness of his son?

We are not told. What we are told is the meaning of that word 'compassion'. 'The Greek verb *splangchnizomai* reveals to us the deep and powerful meaning of this expression. The *splangchna* are the entrails of the body or, as we might say today, the guts. They are the place where our most intimate and intense emotions are located.'[12] In other words, Jesus was painting a picture of a father who hurt 'at gut level' when he saw his son hurting.

Jesus portrays a God whose love is immense, inexhaustible, unfathomable, tender; a God who, far from being 'a distant God, a God to be feared and avoided, a God of revenge,' is a 'God who is moved by our pains and participates in the fullness of the human struggle.'[13] Like a good human father or mother, God wants his children to be happy.

A Project

Reflect on the compassionate father and on Thomas Merton's claim that God is not 'a furious father'[14] seeking to punish or to be avenged but 'a calm sea of mercy'.[15] Think about the way you perceive God and jot down words which you would use to describe him.

A Prayer

I come as myself.
Just as I am.
This moment.
My feelings, my fears
My joys, my sadnesses.
You see me as I really am
You know me
Through and through
You see all
All that I am
Or ever have been.[16]

The Welcoming Father

Yesterday we saw that God to whom we travel is a God of compassion. When we hurt, he hurts. When we weep, he weeps. Today we continue to focus on the father in Jesus' parable. He helps us to understand what God is like.

Even when his son was a long way from home, Jesus tells us, this father saw his son, felt for him and then did a most extraordinary thing: 'his father . . . ran.' (Luke 15:20)

This pen picture would have astonished the crowds who first heard Jesus' story. An Eastern father rarely runs. The climate is too hot for one thing. Running is considered to lack dignity, for another. Yet Jesus paints a picture of a man so anxious to be united with his son that he gathers up his long robes and races at great speed to greet the boy who had turned his back on home.

The picture was intended to convey the truly good news that it is 'not that I am stumbling towards the Abba Father, but that the Abba Father is running towards me. It is not that I love God but that God loves me, not that I believe in God but that God believes in me . . . the divine love is contemplating me. He sees me and understands and accepts me.'[17] He has compassion on me. He creates me afresh from moment to moment. He protects me.

God is the God who comes. But his many comings often go undetected because he frequently comes disguised and hidden in the ordinary, everyday things of life:

> *I was awakened by a tiny gleam of light*
> *it slipped through my curtain, onto my face.*
> *It drew me to my feet and on to the window*

Drawing back the curtains
dawn stepped softly into my room.
I knew it was God.

In the middle of my loneliness
the phone rang.
A voice I knew so well, said
'Hello, I love you.'
Love stirred in my soul
I knew that it was God.

Rain fell gently on the thirsty ground.
Slowly, carefully, steadily it came
to an earth parched with waiting.
Through those holy raindrops
I walked, unafraid—without an umbrella.
I knew that it was God . . .

It was only a Silver Maple
but in the morning's sunlight
it was filled with heaven.
I stood in a trance
as one touched by angel wings.
I knew that it was God.[18]

A Project

Recall occasions when God has come to you: when you have experienced his love or felt his presence. If your mind draws a blank, think back over the past twenty-four hours. Recall the good things that happened to you. Recognize them for what they are—gifts from the God who comes. Thank him for them.

A Prayer

Come, Lord Jesus (Revelation 22:20)

A Thought for This Week

God is Emmanuel
God-with-us

The Forgiving Father

In Charles Dickens' *David Copperfield*, there is a moving description of love for the lost. Emily has run away and Mr Peggotty announces that he is going 'through all the wureld' to search for her. But: 'Every night as reg'lar as the night comes, the candle must be stood in its old pane of glass, that if ever she should see it, it may seem to say, "Come back, my child, come back." '[19]

The lost son in Jesus' story did come back. He came back rehearsing his speech. But his speech did not begin with 'Forgive', it began with 'Father':

> *Father, I have sinned against both heaven and you, and am no longer worthy of being called your son . . .*

(Luke 15:19 LB)

The son knew that he had forfeited his right to the privileges of home and sonship. The father knew that he had every right to punish the son who had abused his love. But the father chose not to exercise his right. Instead, he stepped out of the realm of rights and into the realm of grace. Grace is a generous, free gift which the giver need not give but which often melts the heart of the receiver. This gesture proved that the father had already let go of any bitterness or hurt, anger or hatred he may have once felt. Even before his son could stammer out his confession, the father had already forgiven him. For 'to forgive' means 'to let go', 'to drop', 'to release'.

In describing a father who expressed such forgiveness tangibly: 'His father . . . embraced him and kissed him' (Luke 15:20), Jesus seems to have been anxious to persuade us that God is not a God who extracts from his people remorse for their misdeeds. God is a God whose love is the candle in the window, who longs to let us off the hook, to release us from our past as hostages are set free from their captors, to liberate us from ourselves as prisoners are set free from prison, to pour into us the same kind of energy which adrenalin gives to athletes when they hear the starting pistol at the beginning of a race: the energy to come home.

A Project

Think about this claim: the only way we can come to God is just as we are, 'sinful, spiritually handicapped and disabled in many ways, chronic patients'.[20] We must learn to accept these handicaps and disabilities, because God accepts us as we are and loves us as we are.

A Prayer

> Just as I am . . .
> O Lamb of God
> I come.

With Jesus in the Wilderness

Jesus, full of the Holy Spirit, returned from the Jordan and was led by the Spirit in the desert, where for forty days he was tempted by the devil. He ate nothing during those days, and at the end of them he was hungry.

The devil said to him, 'If you are the Son of God, tell this stone to become bread.'

Jesus answered, 'It is written: "Man does not live on bread alone."'

The devil led him up to a high place and showed him in an instant all the kingdoms of the world. And he said to him, 'I will give you all their authority and splendour, for it has been given to me, and I can give it to anyone I want to. So if you worship me, it will all be yours.'

Jesus answered, 'It is written: "Worship the Lord your God and serve him only."'

The devil led him to Jerusalem and had him stand on the highest point of the temple. 'If you are the Son of God,' he said, 'throw yourself down from here. For it is written:

> *"He will command his angels*
> *concerning you*
> *to guard you carefully;*
> *they will lift you up in their hands,*
> *so that you will not strike your foot*
> *against a stone."'*

Jesus answered, 'It says: "Do not put the Lord your God to the test."'
When the devil had finished all this tempting, he left him until an opportune time.

(Luke 4:1–13 NIV)

The Tragedy of Sin

Last week we saw how the prodigal son enjoyed a brand new start and experienced new joy when he returned to his father. We also saw that God is good. We need to remind ourselves of that as we continue on our journey.

This week, before we journey into the wilderness with Jesus, we attempt to trace sin to its root. To do so, we examine one of the readings for the first Sunday in Lent where we see God's enemy, Satan, sidle up to Eve:

> *Now the snake was the most cunning animal that the Lord God had made. The snake asked the woman, 'Did God really tell you not to eat fruit from any tree in the garden?'*
>
> *'We may eat the fruit of any tree in the garden,' the woman answered, 'except the tree in the middle of it. God told us not to eat the fruit of that tree or even touch it; if we do, we will die.'*
>
> *The snake replied, 'That's not true; you will not die. God said that because he knows that when you eat it you will be like God and know what is good and what is bad.'*
>
> *The woman saw how beautiful the tree was and how good its fruit would be to eat, and she thought how wonderful it would be to become wise. So she took some of the fruit and ate it.*
>
> (Genesis 3:1–6 GNB)

God is not a spoil-sport. He is good. He therefore had a good reason for placing one tree out of bounds. The reason was that it is God's right to decide what is good and what is evil. It is his prerogative to determine what is best for us and what will prove harmful. In forbidding Adam and Eve to eat from the tree, he was asking them to trust him and to depend on him. But he did not force them into obedience. He gave them a free choice. And because Adam and Eve found the gifts of God more attractive than God himself, they chose independence. They refused to believe their Creator and trusted his enemy instead.

Here we have the tap root of sin. Sin does not stem from acts of disobedience. Sin is far more subtle and serious than that. Sin places self at the centre of the universe instead of God. Sin revolves around self instead of around God. Sin seeks self-glorification rather than the glory of God. The tragedy of sin is that it views God with suspicion. It does not allow God to be God. It rejects his love. The 'very hands outstretched to save us are seen as hands reaching out to unseat us.'[21]

A Project

Think about the society in which we live. Think of individuals whose lives clearly revolve around themselves instead of around God. Think of groups of people who seek their own glory by drawing attention to themselves and their own worth instead of pointing others to the glory of God. Think of occasions when you have said 'no' to God and therefore, by implication, have said 'yes' to yourself. Then look at a picture of Christ dying on the Cross. Recall the reason he is hanging there: that God loved his world so much that he sacrificed his one and only Son (see John 3:16).

A Prayer

Lord, draw me until my whole being revolves around you.

The Seriousness of Sin

We saw yesterday that when Adam and Eve were put to the test they failed, in that they deliberately refused to allow God to be God. We saw that to displace God is what sin is. None of us can point the finger at Adam or Eve. As Paul reminds us, we are just like them: 'All have sinned and fall short of the glory of God.' (Romans 3:23)

The consequences, as Paul also tells us, are far-reaching. As a result of Adam and Eve's bias to sin, 'death has spread to the whole human race because everyone has sinned.' (Romans 5:12)

I sometimes picture it like this. When God made his wonderful world, it was as though he crafted a beautiful boat for the first couple and invited them to explore their surroundings. He warned them that certain coves were guarded by submerged rocks; to venture in their vicinity was to court disaster—even death. The couple enjoyed cruising in their boat whose engine was fuelled by energy derived from oil.

But one day, they were lured into one of the forbidden coves. The boat was speared by a sharp rock whereupon a thick, slimy oil slick seeped from the engine-room onto the turquoise sea, coating the rocks, saturating the sand, sticking to the sea-gulls and killing the dolphins. The couple applied the best detergent they could find but they were incapable of rescuing the birds and the animals, the beaches and their boat. Everything was polluted.

When God saw what had happened he was filled with horror and indignation at the destruction of his creation. The couple became boat builders, but every boat they made was flawed. Oil oozed from each one, further polluting every part of God's world.

God mounted a rescue operation. He sent his Son into the world. In his life, he showed the couple and their descendents how to deal a death-blow to the disease which had spread to the whole of the human race. When he died, his shed blood became an effective, well-proved detergent in dealing with the gigantic oil slick. As Paul sums up the situation, many people died because of the sin of Adam. 'But God's grace is much greater' (Romans 5:15). Through Jesus he 'sets all mankind free', restoring to them the ability and desire to place God in the centre of their universe.

A Project

Reflect on your journey through life: past and present. Reflect on your thoughts and attitudes as well as your actions. Recall occasions when poison has flowed from you and further polluted our world. Thank God that 'his grace is greater' than your failure which contributes to the world's failure, and that he has come to set you and the world free.

A Prayer

> Search me, O God, and know my heart;
> test me and know my . . . thoughts.
> See if there is any offensive way in me,
> and lead me in the way everlasting.

> (Psalm 139:23–24)

The Purpose of Temptation

We saw yesterday that one of the reasons Jesus came to live among us was to show us how to deal with the disease which has spread to every member of the human race; how to live a life which gives God his rightful place. That does not mean that he escaped temptation.

As the writer to the Hebrews reminds us, he was tempted just as we are, but he never sinned (Hebrews 4:15). That is why, for the rest of this week, we shall walk with Jesus into the wilderness and watch the way he handled temptation:

> *Jesus, full of the Holy Spirit, returned from the Jordan and was led by the Spirit in the desert, where for forty days he was tempted by the devil.*

(Luke 4:1)

Jesus had just been baptised. Before his public ministry was launched, the wind of the Spirit blew him into the wilds where, for forty days he was tempest-tossed. Tempted.

When the word 'temptation' is used in the New Testament it means 'testing'. Jesus was now confronted with the same choice Adam and Eve once faced. He could do God's work in God's way, or in his own way. As he sidled alongside God's Son, Satan doubtless hoped that, like Adam and Eve, Jesus would refuse to allow God to be God; that he would choose independence rather than God-dependence; that he would disbelieve God's Word rather than stake his life on it. God, on the other hand, allowed Jesus to go through this time of turbulence so that the quality of his faith and commitment would be exposed and strengthened. This is precisely what happened. As St Luke reminds us, Jesus emerged from his ordeal in the desert 'in the power of the Spirit'

(Luke 4:14)—like a beautiful race horse galloping towards his goal. Over the next three days we shall examine some of the reasons why Jesus succeeded where we so often fail.

A Project

Think about some of the ways you have been tempted recently. Were there occasions when, through the testing, you were clearly strengthened in your faith and commitment, helped to mature, or purified in some way? Were there other times when, like Adam and Eve, you refused to allow God to be God? What happened? Talk to God out of the experience.

A Prayer

Make this prayer your own if you can:

> Almighty God,
> whose Son Jesus Christ fasted forty days in the wilderness,
> and was tempted as we are, yet without sin:
> give us grace to discipline ourselves
> in obedience to your Spirit;
> and, as you know our weakness,
> so may we know your power to save;
> through Jesus Christ our Lord.[22]

A Thought for This Week

> Temptation is not the same as sin. It can't be. Jesus was tempted but he never sinned.

Jesus' Secret

One of the reasons why Jesus emerged from the wilderness empowered by the Spirit rather than defeated by Satan was that he had a motto which governed his life-style: 'Your will, not mine.' When Satan tempted Jesus in the wilderness, his will was thwarted by this cast-iron life-motto:

> *Jesus returned from the Jordan full of the Holy Spirit and was led by the Spirit into the desert, where he was tempted by the Devil for forty days. In all that time he ate nothing, so that he was hungry when it was over.*
>
> *The Devil said to him, 'If you are God's Son, order this stone to turn into bread.'*
>
> *But Jesus answered, 'The scripture says, "Man cannot live on bread alone."'*

(Luke 4:1–4)

Satan or Lucifer, 'the light bearer', as he is sometimes called, had once been God's servant. But spiritual pride caused him to rebel against God, the source of the light he carried. Cast out of God's presence, he became the source of the spiritual pride which beguiles us. When he tests us, his aim is to persuade us to displace God. Knowing our weaknesses, he also knows now best to attack us. Watch him assault Jesus.

Jesus had been fasting for forty days in countryside where the ground was littered with large, flat, cream-coloured stones which look like pitta bread. Sensing Jesus' hunger, Satan evidently hoped that, just as he had persuaded Adam and Eve to taste the forbidden fruit, so he would be able to entice the Son of God to use his miraculous powers to turn these bread-like stones into much-needed food. Unlike Adam and Eve, Jesus refused to capitulate. Instead, the temptation seemed to strengthen and clarify his life's goal. He would not live or use his God-entrusted gifts for meeting his own needs, no matter how pressing these were. He would say a constant and continual 'yes' to his Father.

We all have a motto which governs the way we live. Our motto reveals our attitude to God, and determines the choices we make on our journey through life.

A Project

Ask yourself, 'What is my motto?' Write it down. Look at it. Does it need spring-cleaning, or replacing with one which matches the motto of Jesus more closely?

A Prayer

> O Jesus, I have promised
> To serve Thee to the end;
> Be Thou for ever near me,
> My Master and my Friend:
> I shall not fear the battle
> If Thou art by my side,
> Nor wander from the pathway
> If Thou wilt be my Guide.
>
> O let me feel Thee near me:
> The world is ever near;
> I see the sights that dazzle,
> The tempting sounds I hear;
> My foes are ever near me,
> Around me and within;
> But, Jesus, draw Thou nearer,
> And shield my soul from sin.[23]

One of Satan's Ploys

Yesterday, we noticed how Satan attempted to persuade Jesus to use his God-given gifts to meet his own pressing needs. We observed how Jesus' motto released him so that, like an arrow, he went straight for his life's target: to serve God and not self. To say 'yes' to his Father. This same motto, 'your will, not mine,' gave him a sense of direction and drive when Satan struck for the second time:

> *Then the Devil took him up and showed him in a second all the kingdoms of the world. 'I will give you all this power and all this wealth,' the Devil told him. 'It has been handed over to me, and I can give it to anyone I choose. All this will be yours, then, if you worship me.'*
>
> *Jesus answered, 'The scripture says, "Worship the Lord your God and serve only him!"'*

(Luke 4:5–8)

When Satan dangled the apple of being as wise as God in front of Eve, she refused to resist rebelling against God. She was power-hungry. When Satan offered similar power to Jesus, he rejected it and in doing so reinforced his life's motto. He underlined his resolve that neither his own needs nor his own rights, neither the pursuit of pleasure nor the flattery of power should govern his actions. He had come to do his Father's will: 'When Christ was about to come into the world, he said to God: "Here I am, to do your will, O God."' (See Hebrews 10:7)

Once again Jesus passed the test with flying colours and, in doing so, showed us how to conquer temptation when we meet it on our journey. We, too, will be tempted to be guided by our own needs or apparent rights, to live for pleasure and to thirst for power and prestige. Left to ourselves and tempted by the lure of such seeming attractions, we shall find ourselves as stubborn as Eve. We must therefore depend, not on our own strength but on the help Jesus offers. We need him to be our Saviour. Having been tempted just like us, he understands our frailty and comes to our aid whenever we call.

A Project

Think back over some of the choices you have made in your life—both large and small. Notice where you made a particular choice because you were wanting to promote the Kingdom of God and serve its King. Notice, too, where you were promoting the kingdom of self—living for pleasure or longing for power or prestige. Think, too, of times when Jesus has strengthened you in times of testing, and thank him.

A Prayer

> Lord Jesus Christ, Son of God,
> have mercy on me,
> a sinner.

Choices on the Journey

Will my life revolve around me: my needs and wants, my right to power and prestige? Or will I allow my life to be governed by my motto: 'your will, not mine?' Will I cling to the reins of my life or will I hand the controls over to God? These are the choices Jesus faced in the wilderness. They are the questions Adam and Eve also faced in Paradise. And they are the questions which face us as we continue on our journey. We discover the reality of our reactions to them when temptation comes our way. That is why temptation can either strengthen us or bring about our downfall.

Even when we have determined that, like Jesus, our lives will revolve around God and be dedicated to the extension of his Kingdom, times of testing will come, as they did to Jesus:

> *Then the Devil took him to Jerusalem and set him on the highest point of the Temple, and said to him, 'If you are God's Son, throw yourself down from here. For the scripture says, "God will order his angels to take good care of you." It also says, "They will hold you up with their hands so that not even your feet will be hurt on the stones." ' But Jesus answered, 'The scripture says, "Do not put the Lord your God to the test." '*

(Luke 4:9–12)

In refusing to act recklessly, expecting God to rescue him, Jesus was underlining the choice he had already made: to allow God to call the tune. In reversing the choice of Adam and Eve in this way, Jesus leaves us with an example and an assurance. He shows us and assures us that we need not cave in to the gravitational pull of power or popularity, prestige or possessions, however attractive they may seem. Whether their tug comes from within or without, we can say a persistent 'no' to each of them and a consistent 'yes' to God. And when we fail, we have only to return home like the prodigal.

A Project

Think about recent government policies, current advertisements, trends in the church and your own philosophy of life—outside the church and within the fellowship. Trace the way in which you and others are responding to the perpetual pull of popularity, prestige, possessions and power. Think, too, of people and groups who have resisted this pull and who refuse to make their choices on the basis of 'What's in it for me?' Ask yourself: 'How do I feel about people who swim against the cultural tide in this way? How do I feel about imitating them—and Christ?'

A Prayer

> Batter my heart, three person'd God . . .
> for I
> Except you enthrall me, never shall be free,
> Nor ever chaste, except you ravish me.[24]

Newness of Life

Jesus was alone in the wilderness when he embarked on his pitched battle against evil. At some stage, he must therefore have told his disciples some of the ways in which temptation came to him. We do not know when he told them. Or why. We do know that, at the end of his gruelling test, God made it abundantly clear that he had not deserted his Son but that he was watching and waiting in the wings to send help at the appropriate time: 'the Devil left Jesus; and angels came and helped him.' (Matthew 4:11)

Did Jesus feel abandoned even by his Father during those forty days in the desert? Possibly. When testing times come it can feel as though God is playing hide and seek. But just as God sent his ambassadors to strengthen and support his Son, so Jesus acts on our behalf when we are tested. Like a good trainer, he wills us to win. We can say this with certainty because of the way he warned Peter that just as Satan had attempted to seduce him, so the Enemy desired to devour the disciples: 'Satan has received permission to test all of you but I have prayed for you, Simon, that your faith will not fail.' (Luke 22:32)

From this moving promise we may safely surmise that the reason why Jesus spelt out Satan's strategy against him was that he knew that almost every day we would be tempted similarly. He knew that although the testing would come in a whole variety of disguises, the thrust would be similar on each occasion. We would be tempted to the spiritual pride which persuades us to do what we want instead of what God wants, and because our love of power is innate, we would be lured by the seeming attraction of prestige and possessions instead of by dependency on God. Temptation would attack us as it assaulted him: when we are weak and lonely and through the plausible medium of our common sense. If heeded, it would prevent us from becoming the people God always intended us to be; if resisted, it would help us to journey on with renewed joy and the assurance that we were growing more like Jesus.

A Project

John the Baptist paved the way for Jesus by imploring people to repent. To repent does not mean to grovel guiltily at God's feet. It means to do a U-turn which affects every part of our being: mind, emotions, desire and will. Think back over this week's readings. Ask God to show you where you have felt the pull of power or possessions, pride or prestige. Ask him to change you until your life's aim mirrors that of Jesus.

A Prayer

> Almighty God,
> I have sinned against you in thought and word and deed,
> forgive all that is past
> and grant that I may serve you in newness of life
> for the glory of Jesus.

With Jesus on the Mount of Transfiguration

Eight days later he took Peter, James, and John with him into the hills to pray. And as he was praying, his face began to shine, and his clothes became dazzling white and blazed with light. Then two men appeared and began talking with him—Moses and Elijah! They were splendid in appearance, glorious to see; and they were speaking of his death at Jerusalem, to be carried out in accordance with God's plan.

Peter and the others had been very drowsy and had fallen asleep. Now they woke up and saw Jesus covered with brightness and glory, and the two men standing with him. As Moses and Elijah were starting to leave, Peter, all confused and not even knowing what he was saying, blurted out, 'Master, this is wonderful! We'll put up three shelters—one for you and one for Moses and one for Elijah!'

But even as he was saying this, a bright cloud formed above them; and terror gripped them. And a voice from the cloud said, 'This is my Son, my Chosen One; listen to him.'

Then, as the voice died away, Jesus was there alone with his disciples. They didn't tell anyone what they had seen until long afterwards.

(Luke 9: 28–36 LB)

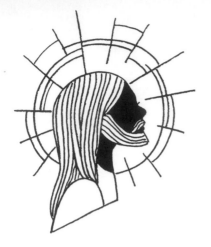

A Glimpse of Glory

This week, as we journey with Jesus, we travel to the Mount of Transfiguration.

Luke sets the scene when he tells of an occasion when Jesus went up into the hills to pray. He took with him three companions: Peter, James and John. While he was praying, his face seemed to change, his clothes seemed to dazzle and he was covered with brightness, shining with glory. Two men suddenly appeared alongside him: Moses and Elijah. The three talked together about Jesus' forthcoming suffering and death.

Despite the wonder of the occasion, the disciples were overcome by sleep. 'Peter and his companions had been in a deep sleep; but when they awoke, they saw his glory.' (Luke 9:32)

The word glory means value or worth. The glory of Jesus means the reality of who he is. To give glory to Jesus means to express the adoration we feel when we recognize who he is.

How did the disciples feel when they rubbed the sleep from their eyes and saw the startling scene? They had caught occasional glimpses of Jesus' glory before. (See, for example, John 2:11.) The reality of who Jesus was, the exact image of God, seems sometimes to have shone through his humanity. Just as the disciples were simply seeing what had always been there, so God wants us to witness his worth; to gaze on his glory and to let this be the springboard of our worship.

That is why he begs us to move out of the fast lane from time to time, to be still, to know that he is God. For just as it is those who stop to stare who enjoy to the full the splendours of Spring: the catkins and the pussy willows, the dawn chorus and the scent of the primrose, so it is those who will slow down whose eyes will be opened to the wonder of God;

whose hearts will be filled with the awe which gives rise to true adoration. As St Augustine put it:

> *We shall rest and we shall see*
> *We shall see and we shall love*
> *We shall love and we shall praise.*[25]

A Project

Imagine that, like Peter, James and John, you had been privileged to be with Jesus on the Mount of Transfiguration. Imagine that you had watched glory stream from his face. How might you have felt? What kind of response might you have wanted to make? What kind of reaction does it produce in you now?

A Prayer

> May my resting result in a beholding
> My beholding give birth to adoration
> And my adoration give rise to heartfelt praise
>   and thanksgiving.

More Glimpses of Glory

I once climbed the Mount of Transfiguration, and as I sat in the sun on the plateau where it is believed Jesus was transfigured, I tried to imagine the disciples witnessing Jesus resplendent in glory, and how I might have felt if I had been privileged to be there. I wandered into the chapel which has been built on that mountain top and I was acutely aware that this was holy ground; a place where people become 'lost in wonder, love and praise', a place where people struggle to express the depth of their devotion to God.

Even the God-given gift of the imagination affords us only a hint of the wonder the disciples witnessed on the mountain. But the reality of God is not hidden from us. As Isaiah reminds us: 'The whole earth is full of his glory.' (Isaiah 6:3)

There on the Mount of Transfiguration, the world seemed not simply full, but overflowing with God's glory. I saw it in the deep blue of the sky. I felt it in the warmth of the sun. I heard it in the praises of the pilgrims. I sensed it in the grandeur of the mountains. I touched it in the blades of grass and in the wild flowers. On that memorable day, I realized that the whole earth is full of that which enables us to know God with a heart-knowledge which prompts us to worship him, delight in him and to 'joy in God for his own sake.' [26]

A Project

Evelyn Underhill once made this comment on that verse from Isaiah:

'The **whole earth** is full of Thy glory.' **Full**.

The glory . . . fills not only heaven but earth, the jungle city,
the church and market place, the ballroom and the hospital,
the most sordid and disheartening spheres of service, the roads
humming with traffic and the silent mountains where tiny
plants in exquisite beauty flower for God.[27]

Think about this claim. Ask yourself: 'Where and when have I witnessed the glory of God?' Look for glimpses of God's glory today.

A Prayer

Let all that is within me cry glory.
Glory to the Lord God Most High.

Thought for This Week

Glory comes wrapped in the ordinary:
a spider web, wearing the morning's dew
a mistake, reflected upon and learned from . . .
an autumn tree letting go of her leaves
a spring tree putting leaves on again
a wound, embraced and understood.[28]

Full of God's Glory

Originally, the people who observed Lent were new converts to Christianity. Since they were all to be baptised together on Easter Day, Lent formed the final part of their Baptism preparation. The Lent readings included the story of the Transfiguration to show these young Christians that just as the likeness of his Father shone through the humanity of Jesus and transformed him, because the Holy Spirit lives in us and is at work in us, we can also be changed. Paul uses powerful picture language to help us to understand: 'You are a Temple of the Holy Spirit' (1 Corinthians 3:16); 'We have this glory in earthen vessels.' (2 Corinthians 4:5,6,7 JB)

As a friend of mine once put it:

> *In Jesus, the glory came in the ordinary.*
> *In us, the ordinary is wrapped around the glory.*

Or, as someone else has expressed the inexpressible:

> *In this frail envelope of our body is enclosed a great marvel.*[29]

Making reference to this same marvel, Thomas Merton wrote:

> *Make ready for the Christ,*
> *Whose smile,*
> *like lightning,*
> *Sets free the song of everlasting glory*
> *That now sleeps,*
> *in your paper flesh,*
> *like dynamite.*[30]

A Project

Jesus tells us that he stands outside the door of our life waiting to be invited in (See Revelation 3:20). When his life fills us, he transforms us and his glory shines through us. Imagine that, to-day, he literally knocks on your front door. You let him into your home, take him on a conducted tour, invite him to take up residence there. How does it feel to have the King of Glory living with you? Can you hand over the keys of your life as well as your home to him? Talk to God about your reactions—the things you find difficult as well as the things which seem easier.

A Prayer

Make this prayer your own:

> Take me and all I have,
> do with me whatever you will.
> Send me where you will.
> Use me as you will.
> I surrender myself and all I possess,
> absolutely and entirely,
> unconditionally and forever,
> to your control.[31]

Changed Into God's Likeness

On the Mount of Transfiguration, Jesus glowed with glory. The earliest Christians were taught that they could also be changed 'from glory into glory'; that just as Jesus reflected his Father's glory (Hebrews 1:3), so we can reflect Jesus' glory. As Paul puts it: 'All of us who are Christians . . . reflect like mirrors the glory of the Lord.' (2 Corinthians 3:18)

If we are to be like a mirror reflecting the glory of God, it follows that we must turn towards him and take time to contemplate him. Such contemplation reaps amazing rewards. To quote Paul again:

> *We are transfigured by the Spirit of the Lord in ever-increasing splendour into His own image.*
>
> (2 Corinthians 3:18 JBP)

In other words, we become God's ikon.

John Powell, Associate Professor at Loyola University, testifies from personal experience that when God's Spirit effects such changes in us, we may enjoy a surge of spiritual new life which can only be likened to springtime. He describes what happened when he did the project which I suggested at the end of yesterday's reading—inviting Jesus into the house of his life.

> *From the early morning shower till the darkened moments while waiting for sleep, I kept inviting Jesus into my house of many rooms. I kept reassuring Him that I was ready to admit my own [spiritual] bankruptcy, my own helplessness to direct my life, to find peace and joy . . .*

What began to happen to me almost immediately can be compared only to springtime. It seemed as though I had been through a long, hard-frozen wintertime. My heart and soul had suffered all the barrenness, the nakedness of nature in winter. Now in this springtime of the Spirit, it seemed as though the veins of my soul were thawing, as though blood was beginning to course through my soul again. New foliage and new beauty began to appear in me and around me . . .

I knew with an imperturbable inner certainty that my loving God had touched me![32]

A Project

Ask God to show you if there is any way in which he would like you to change this Lent. Ask him to bring about for you a springtime of the Spirit.

A Prayer

> Breathe on me, Breath of God;
> Fill me with life anew,
> That I may love what Thou dost love,
> And do what Thou wouldst do.
>
> Breathe on me, Breath of God,
> Till I am wholly Thine,
> Until this earthly part of me
> Glows with Thy fire divine.[33]

Aglow with JESUS

Thursday

Reflecting God's Glory

Just as on the Mount of Transfiguration, and at other times, the divinity of Jesus shone through his humanity, so God's glory beams through the faces and actions of those who are being transformed into his likeness.

People like Malcolm Muggeridge have been astonished by this when working with Mother Teresa of Calcutta:

> When I first set eyes on her—the occasion a casual TV interview—I at once realized that I was in the presence of someone of unique quality. This was not due to her appearance, which is homely and unassuming, so that words like 'charm' or 'charisma' do not apply. Nor to her shrewdness and quick understanding, though these are very marked . . . There is a phrase in one of the psalms that always, for me, evokes her presence: 'the beauty of holiness'—that special beauty, amounting to a kind of pervasive luminosity generated by a life dedicated wholly to loving God and His creation.[34]

Others speaking of Mother Teresa say that when she receives Holy Communion, she glows; that the same glory is glimpsed when she holds in her arms one of God's dying people, rescued from the gutters of Calcutta.

Mother Teresa would be the first to insist that if God's glory shines through her it can shine through all who contemplate Christ. The transfigured Christ whose light blazes in her is the same Christ who lights the dark corners of our lives. The more our lives revolve, not around self but around the Light of the World, Jesus, the more others will sense his presence even in us: 'Christ in you, the hope of glory.' (Colossians 1:27)

A Project

Recall occasions when you have seen the glory of God beaming through a person or people. Where was it? What happened? What effect did it have on you?

A Prayer

Dear Jesus,
help us to spread your fragrance everywhere we go.
Flood our souls with your spirit and life.
Penetrate and possess our whole being so utterly that our lives
may only be a radiance of yours.
Shine through us, and be so in us that every soul we come in contact with
may feel your presence in our soul.
Let them look up and see no longer us but only Jesus!
Stay with us, and then we shall begin to shine as you shine;
so to shine as to be a light to others;
the light, O Jesus, will be all from you, none of it will be ours:
it will be you, shining on others through us.
Let us thus praise you in the way you love best
by shining on those around us.[35]

Thought for This Week

The one and only test of work or the life of prayer is the extent to which they reflect that pure glory of God.[36]

Hints of Grief and Glory

The sun shone from a cloudless sky one evening as I set out on a lengthy car journey. As I drove, dark clouds scudded across the sky obscuring the sun. But gradually, the sun seemed to burn a hole in the clouds and suddenly the sky was ablaze with glory: the black clouds revealing their silver lining, the sun sending out streamers of gold which spread their light over the sleeping fields.

The scene reminded me of the Transfiguration where the picture of splendour and majesty is mixed with references to pain and death. As Luke puts it, Jesus was not the only one to glow on the mountain-top. Moses, the Lawgiver and Elijah, the Prophet were similarly resplendent in glory, yet 'they talked with Jesus about the way in which he would soon fulfil God's purpose by dying in Jerusalem.' (Luke 9:31 GNB)

Perhaps this mixture of splendour and sorrow should not surprise us? As Jesus reminded his friends on the first Easter Day: 'Wasn't it precisely predicted by the prophets that the Messiah would have to suffer . . . before entering his time of glory?' (Luke 24:26)

History also suggests that pain and glory frequently go together in the life of the believer. They went together for Francis of Assisi. One memorable day, he was given the privilege of seeing a vision of a six-winged seraph who approached him 'out of the blue'. As the seraph came close, it became evident that he looked like a man whose body bore the hall-marks of suffering: his hands, feet and side were still scarred. Francis' encounter with the Crucified, Risen Christ was so intimate that day that when he came out of his trance, his body was scarred like his Master's. His moment of greatest glory was also a time of the most intense pain.

A Project

Think about Jesus' mysterious words: 'The hour has now come for the Son of Man to receive great glory. I am telling you the truth: a grain of wheat remains no more than a single grain unless it is dropped into the ground and dies. If it does die, then it produces many grains' (John 12:23,24 GNB).

Think about the Living Bible's translation of that verse:

> *Jesus replied that the time had come for him to return to his glory in heaven, and that 'I must fall and die like a grain of wheat that falls between the furrows of the earth. Unless I die I will be alone—a single seed. But my death will produce many new wheat kernels—a plentiful harvest of new lives. If you love your life down here—you will lose it. If you despise your life down here—you will exchange it for eternal glory.'*

A Prayer

> Lord Jesus Christ,
> I would come to You,
> Live my life for You,
> Son of God.
> All Your commands I know are true,
> Your many gifts will make me new,
> Into my life Your power breaks through,
> Living Lord.[37]

Turn it into Glory

Pain and glory often go together. We observed this yesterday as we continued to keep our eyes on the transfigured Christ. The same message throbs through life. It was underlined for me once when I read a story about a young woman suffering from cystic fibrosis, a disease which affects the organs of the body, including the lungs, and which shortens drastically the life-expectation of the sufferer. Just before this young woman, Peggy, was admited to the hospital where she died, aged 21, she took as her motto a quotation from William Barclay: 'Endurance is not just the ability to bear a hard thing, but to turn it into glory.'[38]

This gave birth to a resolve. She would turn into glory whatever she was called upon to suffer in the days leading up to her death. She challenged her mother to do the same.

I have seen patients dying of cancer ablaze with the glory of God. I have seen God's glory transform the face of those entrusted with prolonged and crippling pain. It is a moving and humbling experience.

It must have been even more humbling for Peter, James and John to see Jesus' face change and his clothing become 'brilliant as lightning'. Humbling, too, to hear Jesus, Moses and Elijah 'appearing in glory' but 'speaking of his death at Jerusalem'. And it must have been moving to observe the penitent thief become so aware of Jesus' glory on the cross that he was prompted to pray: 'Jesus, remember me when you come into your Kingdom' (Luke 23:42), to hear the centurion exclaim as Jesus died: 'Truly this was the Son of God' (Matthew 27:54).

A Project

Picture, as vividly as you can, the transfigured Jesus. Picture, too, Jesus hanging from the Cross with the thieves beside him and the centurion watching him. Let your mind and imagination move from one picture to the other. Pray out of the experience.

A Prayer

You revealed your glory to the disciples to strengthen them for the scandal of the cross. Grant us the grace to see your glory that we may be strengthened to give glory to you in everything: times of joy and times of pain.

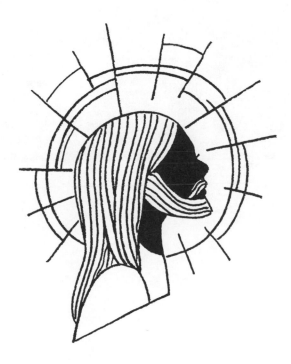

Journey to Jerusalem

When the hour came, Jesus took his place at the table with the apostles. He said to them, 'I have wanted so much to eat this Passover meal with you before I suffer! For I tell you, I will never eat it until it is given its full meaning in the Kingdom of God.'

Then Jesus took a cup, gave thanks to God, and said, 'Take this and share it among yourselves. I tell you that from now on I will not drink this wine until the Kingdom of God comes.'

Then he took a piece of bread, gave thanks to God, broke it, and gave it to them, saying, 'This is my body, which is given for you. Do this in memory of me.' In the same way, he gave them the cup after the supper, saying, 'This cup is God's new covenant sealed with my blood, which is poured out for you.'

(Luke 22:14–20 GNB)

Joy on the Journey

After the Transfiguration, we frequently read that 'Jesus knew every-thing that was going to happen to him' (John 18:4). We also read that his disciples did not understand when he tried to warn them that he was about to suffer, die and rise again. When the people with whom we live and work fail to understand the nature of our calling, life can become very lonely. So that journey from Galilee to Jerusalem must have been laced with loneliness for Jesus. Until he met Zacchaeus—the tiny, tree-climbing tax-collector, who was determined to catch a glimpse of the healer he had heard so much about.

Zacchaeus' eagerness must have brought joy to Jesus. Jesus, in turn, brought spring-like joy to Zacchaeus: he stopped to acknowledge Zacchaeus' presence, called him by name, visited his home and struck up a relationship which resulted in the turning of the tide of Zacchaeus' life.

Luke hints that, like most employees of the Romans, Zacchaeus was a crook: greedy, fraudulent and ruthless. And he was hated. But while Jesus was with him Zacchaeus vowed: 'I will give half my belongings to the poor, and if I have cheated anyone, I will pay him back four times as much' (Luke 19:8). Jesus' response to this vow was a triumphant one: 'Salvation has come to this house today.' (Luke 19:9)

The word 'salvation' means, among other things, deliverance from disease; so it implies health and wholeness. It also means rescue from the power and guilt of sin. And, of course, one of Jesus' titles is 'Saviour', the One who will save us from our sin. So quite literally 'salvation' had come to Zacchaeus' house: he had been set free from the greed which had held him in its grip for so long, delivered from the desire to live for self, released to serve others, and he had entertained in his own home the Saviour of the world.

Jesus went on to explain that the reason he had come to earth was to seek and to save the lost (Luke 19:10). Zacchaeus had been lost in the sense that he had lived like a traveller who had lost his way. He had been lost in the sense that he was like a man riddled with disease. He had not only been found, he had been made new. Jesus must therefore have gone on his way strengthened in his resolve to go on searching for the Zacchaeuses of this world, and to go on loving them, even though it would cost him his life.

A Project

For Zacchaeus, Jesus' presence was like the Spring sunshine—it drew from him all the good which Jesus saw buried deep within him. Ask God to draw from the soil of your life the fruit of the Spirit: love, joy, peace, patience, kindness, goodness, self control. (Galatians 5:22–23)

A Prayer

Holy Spirit, fall upon me afresh . . .
Enable me to do now those things which before were impossible.[39]

A Response of Love to Love

When a person opens their heart to others in the way Jesus offered himself as he carried on searching for 'the lost', they give others a peculiar power over them: the power to accept or reject their love. When the self-gift is accepted, they are filled with a sense of well-being and joy. A few days after Zacchaeus sent Jesus on his way rejoicing, Mary of Bethany also brought him joy and encouragement.

Like many women at that time, Mary appears to have acquired for herself some very expensive perfume. Some think she may have been keeping it for her Wedding Day. But it would seem that, just as Jesus had warned his disciples that he was soon to die (see Matthew 16:21), so he let Mary into his secret. Maybe these were the deep secrets he shared with her while she sat at his feet?

Six days before the Passover Feast where Jesus was to inaugurate the Last Supper, a special public Sabbath-day supper seems to have been arranged in Bethany. The celebrity guest was Jesus. Did Mary's intuition tell her that this was the last meal she would eat with the one she loved? We are not told. Putting together Matthew and John's description of this meal, we are told that while Jesus was eating, Mary came in clutching 'a bottle of very expensive perfume, and poured it over his head.' She then poured some of it on Jesus' feet and 'wiped them with her hair. The sweet smell of the perfume filled the whole house.' (John 12:3 and Matthew 26:7)

Mary's generous gesture met with a barrage of criticism from the disciples—especially Judas, who asked accusingly: 'Why wasn't this perfume sold for three hundred silver coins and the money given to the poor?' (John 12:5). Jesus, on the other hand, dismissed the criticism, and paid a memorable and most moving tribute to Mary's expressed love: 'It is a fine and beautiful thing she has done for me . . . What she did was to pour this perfume on my body to get me ready for burial.' (Matthew 26:10,12)

A Project

Ask yourself: 'How can I show Jesus that I love him?'

A Prayer

> Lord, may I do something beautiful for you.
> Show me how . . .

Thought for This Week

> Unlike Mary, we cannot minister personally to the human Jesus. We can demonstrate our love for him, however, by helping others in need. As Jesus himself reminded us, when we feed the hungry or give drink to the thirsty, welcome the stranger or provide shelter for the homeless, when we give clothes to those who cannot afford to buy them or visit people in prison, when we care for the sick, the lonely, the bereaved, we are strengthening and loving him. (See Matthew 25:34–40)

Jesus Weeps over Jerusalem

During Lent one year I was on retreat in the Holy Land. On Palm Sunday, my husband and I attended a service which started on the beach by the Sea of Galilee. Here, believers from many nations were handed branches broken from nearby palm trees. Carrying our palms, we processed into the church singing a word we all understood: 'Hosanna'.

After the service of Holy Communion, my husband and I returned to the beach where we sat in silence, contemplating the beauty of the lake which, like a jewel, sparkled in the sunshine. Later that day we were to travel to the busy, bustling, sun-baked city of Jerusalem. Feeling reluctant to exchange the tranquillity of Galilee for the crowded streets of Jerusalem, my thoughts turned to Jesus. How did he manage to drag himself away from the peace of this place he loved to go up to Jerusalem knowing that there he would be flogged and tortured, mocked and spat upon—then brutally murdered?

I turned the question over in my mind for the rest of the morning. The answer came later as I travelled by bus to Jerusalem. 'Love drove him to Jerusalem—to the Cross.' As Julian of Norwich summed it up, 'Love was his meaning.' Or as Catherine of Siena put it: 'Nails could not have held the God-Man to the Cross had love not held him there.'

On the Sunday of Holy Week, Palm Sunday, the depth of Jesus' love for Jerusalem and its people overflowed in the form of tears. The triumphal entry into Jerusalem had begun. Jesus sat astride the donkey, the crowd thronged him and hailed him as their King. Amid this jubilation, as the procession rounded the corner which affords a magnificent, panoramic view of 'the golden city', Jesus feasted his eyes on Jerusalem and began to cry. 'O Jerusalem, Jerusalem, the city that kills the prophets, and stones all those God sends to her! How often I have wanted to gather your children together as a hen gathers her chicks beneath her wings, but you wouldn't let me.' (Luke 19:41 and Matthew 23:37)

When we open ourselves to others in love, we make ourselves vulnerable. When our love is rejected or thrown back in our face, the hurt can be heart-breaking. And Jesus' heart was already being broken.

A Project

Think of pictures you have seen in magazines or newspapers, or on television, of unrest in Jerusalem and the Middle East. Re-read Jesus' lament.

Try to imagine how he feels as he watches the city he loves still trapped in a spiritual winter. Pray for the peace of Jerusalem and ask God to remind you of occasions when you have spurned his love.

A Prayer

> Lord, there are times when I have spurned your love
> and refused the refuge you offer
> Yet you opened wide your arms on the Cross
> And gave me the grace to come into them
> That there I might find peace, rest
> And the Springtime of my soul.

Silent Support

When Jesus wept over Jerusalem, he was sitting astride a donkey. In the West today, docile donkeys have become objects of scorn and ridicule. Not so in the Middle East. There they are still much-used and much-loved modes of transport and, like all animals, are treated as members of their owner's family. Jesus' entry into Jerusalem on the back of an untrained colt would not have been considered strange. Neither would the donkey's back have seemed an unworthy pulpit for the King of Kings. The surprise factor for the disciples would have been the pre-arranged way in which the donkey had been selected:

> As [Jesus] came near Bethphage and Bethany at the Mount of Olives, he sent two disciples ahead with these instructions: 'Go to the village there ahead of you; as you go in, you will find a colt tied up that has never been ridden. Untie it and bring it here. If someone asks you why you are untying it, tell him that the Master needs it.' They went on their way and found everything just as Jesus had told them. As they were untying the colt, its owners said to them, 'Why are you untying it?' 'The Master needs it,' they answered, and they took the colt to Jesus. Then they threw their cloaks over the animal and helped Jesus get on.

(Luke 19:28–35 GNB)

By Palm Sunday, Jesus seemed to have moved into top gear. He knew that he had only five days left and that he had much to accomplish before he died. He had therefore made careful preparations for his Triumphal Entry into Jerusalem—including the choice of the donkey which was to play a key role in the eventful, carnival day. The prophets had foretold that the Messiah would come using this method of transport: 'Look, your king is coming to you! He is humble and rides on a donkey and on a colt, the foal of a donkey.' (Zechariah 9:9)

And, despite the crowds and the crush, the saddle of cloaks and the noise, the donkey courageously carried the King of Kings into the Holy City. I sometimes wonder what would have happened if the chosen donkey had resisted or rebelled when, for the first time in his life, a man sat on his back. The story would have read very differently.

A Project

Reflect: in *The Donkey's Tale*, Margaret Gray describes how the donkey gave his testimony to a girl who believed herself to be useless. 'A long time ago, in a land far away, a man chose me. Not a dashing white horse, but funny old me . . . He doesn't need another genius—he needs a few donkeys who know they have to depend on his strength—not theirs.'[40]

A Prayer

> Lord, like the donkey I can give you hidden, silent support. Make me willing simply to be the pulpit from which you preach.

Jesus Washes His Disciples' Feet

The carnival was over. Jesus knew that the Jerusalem which had welcomed him with such jubilation was on the brink of rejecting him. Even his disciples would desert him. Because he was aware of this, his aloneness must have deepened as the day before his death dawned. But he refused to withdraw his love from his followers: 'He had always loved those . . . who were his own, and he loved them to the very end.' (John 13:1 GNB)

Before his death, he seemed determined to demonstrate the length and breadth, the height and depth of that love. And he chose the setting of the nation's feast, the Passover Supper, to demonstrate it visually.

The Passover Feast was an annual event when the Jews remembered with gratitude the way God had delivered them. The meal had already begun when Jesus 'rose from the table, took off his outer garment, and tied a towel round his waist. Then he poured some water into a basin and began to wash the disciples' feet and dry them with the towel round his waist.' (John 13:4,5)

If you have ever had your feet washed by someone who loves you, you will know that they can convey considerable warmth by the way they soap, wash, and rinse your flesh, by the way they look into your eyes and wipe tenderly between every toe. We can only imagine the tenderness with which Jesus touched each of these men he had grown to love so deeply.

At first, Peter was scandalized at the thought of his Lord and Master performing this mundane task of foot washing. This was slaves' work. But Jesus insisted. He wanted to etch on their memories the fact that he loved them so much that he wanted to cleanse and deliver them from all their sin and guilt. They were going to need this reassurance in the gruelling, grief-stricken hours between his Crucifixion and Resurrection.

Jesus also wanted to leave them with an example. Just as he had served them, so they were to serve each other and receive such service from each other (John 13:15). This would be a hard lesson for them to learn— a few minutes earlier, these same disciples had been arguing about which of them would be greatest in Christ's Kingdom! (Luke 22:24)

A Project

Think about this claim, and ask God to show you what it might mean for you:

> *He who wraps the heaven in clouds girds Himself with a towel; and He in whose hand is the life of all things kneels down to wash the feet of His servants.* [41]

> *If you wish to follow [Jesus]*
> *you must not try to climb the ladder of success and power,*
> *becoming more and more important.*
> *Instead you must walk down the ladder,*
> *to meet and walk with people . . .*
> *in pain.* [42]

A Prayer

Lay before God the guilt which seems to soil your life, and any memories of past failings which plague you, and pray:

Wash me and I shall be whiter than snow . . .
Create in me a new, clean heart, O God,
filled with clean thoughts and right desires.
Restore to me the joy of my salvation.

(Ps. 51:7,10,12 LB)

The Last Supper

When friends know that they are about to part, they often give meaningful farewell gifts to one another. At the Last Supper, as we observed yesterday, Jesus gave his disciples the gift of the foot-washing. Today, we watch while he gives them an even more memorable gift.

The Passover meal which Jesus was celebrating with his friends was a solemn occasion which every family in Jerusalem would also have been enjoying. It began with a prayer praising God for his deliverance, his guidance and his goodness. Because bread had become the silent symbol of God's faithfulness to Israel, the father of the family would then take the crisp Passover loaf in his hands and break it. Jesus followed this tradition closely. He, too, took the pitta-like loaf in his hands, blessed it and broke it, but as he handed it to his friends, he grafted onto the traditional prayer a supplement of his own: 'Take it and eat it, for this is my body'. Later, again keeping to tradition, he took a cup of wine and gave thanks for it and gave it to them, and then he added, 'Each one drink from it, for this is my blood . . . It is poured out to forgive the sins of multitudes.' (Matthew 26:26–28 LB)

When they stopped to unwrap this farewell gift, the disciples must have been moved and amazed by its contents. For by breaking open the loaf, Jesus was implying that he himself was open to them, offering the whole of himself voluntarily. By giving them his blood, they would have understood him to be offering them his life. When they pondered on the invitation to eat and drink, they would know that he was begging them to receive this self-gift into themselves—that just as when we eat bread, the bread becomes a part of us and when we drink wine, we can feel its warmth circulating round our body, so, in some mysterious way which even the most brilliant mind will never understand, by eating the bread and the wine he offered, they could receive into themselves his life and his cleansing.

They would realize, too, that Jesus' offer to 'take' demanded a response: it was a veiled invitation to them to commit themselves to him and his mission. It is as though he was saying to them, I am offering you the gift of myself. Will you, in return, give yourselves to me?

A Project

Hold a lump of bread. Feel its texture. Smell it. Break it. Then eat it—slowly. Be aware that it is becoming a part of you. Think of Jesus' invitation to 'take and eat'. Think, too, of the wider implications of that invitation, and make your own response.

A Prayer

Pray this prayer slowly and meditatively, pausing to drink in its meaning.

> You are
> bread of life . . .
> sun of my life
> tree of my life
> pearl of my life
> strength of my life
> the soil of my being.[43]

Jesus Loves

Jesus had reached his destination: Jerusalem. He had demonstrated his love for his disciples. Then John recalls that Jesus became deeply troubled and declared openly:

> *'I am telling you the truth—one of you is going to betray me.'*
>
> *John asked, 'Who is it, Lord?'*
>
> *Jesus answered, 'I will dip some bread in the sauce and give it to him; he is the man.' So he took a piece of bread, dipped it, and gave it to Judas . . . As soon as Judas took the bread, Satan entered him. Jesus said to him, 'Be quick about what you are doing!' . . . Judas accepted the bread and went out at once. It was night.*
>
> (John 13: 21, 25–27, 30 GNB)

Jesus then went on to predict the disciples' desertion and Peter's denial:

> *Then Jesus said to them, 'This very night all of you will run away and leave me . . .' Peter spoke up and said to Jesus, 'I will never leave you, even though all the rest do!'*
>
> *Jesus said to Peter, 'I tell you that before the cock crows tonight, you will say three times that you do not know me.'*
>
> *Peter answered, 'I will never say that, even if I have to die with you!'*

All the other disciples said the same thing.

(Matthew 26:31,33–35)

Over the next few days, we shall observe how, even though Jesus was suffering physically, emotionally and spiritually, throughout his ordeal, his concern was not for himself but for others. So it seems reasonable to surmise that the reason why he allowed the depth of his distress to be seen was that he wanted his disciples to know that, though they would desert him, he would not forsake them. His love was unshakeable: 'After I am raised to life, I will go to Galilee ahead of you.' (Matthew 26:32)

Jesus' love would have melted Judas' hardness if Judas had chosen to receive it.

A Project

When Sir Thomas More, an English martyr, was being tried, he looked at the man whose lies had led to his arrest and cried: 'I am sorrier for your perjury than for my peril!' Imagine the scene. Recall Jesus' distress in the Upper Room. Think of the people who have hurt or offended you. Compare your own reaction to that of Jesus and Sir Thomas More and pray out of the experience.

A Prayer

Lord, show me how to love others in the way you loved your disciples—in the way you love me.

The Disciples Disperse

Jesus said to them, 'This very night all of you will run away and leave me, for the scripture says, "God will kill the shepherd, and the sheep of the flock will be scattered." '

(Matthew 26:31 GNB)

The Disciples Begin to Disperse

When Jesus whispered to Judas, 'Be quick about what you are doing' (John 13:27), Judas appears to have made his way to the chief priests. He had already made a pact with them—to betray Jesus in exchange for thirty silver coins. Now he fulfilled his part of the bargain by offering to lead Jesus' sworn enemies to the place where Jesus was about to retreat to pray.

For centuries, Christians have clearly been scandalized by this act of treachery. Bible Commentators have called Judas 'a shameful villain'. Even today, on Easter Saturday evening some churches continue to burn an effigy of 'Iniquitous Iscariot'. Judas is the one who 'falls away from the light and accepts the darkness'[44], who 'sells Him that is above all price'[45], who, 'in exchange for money' rejects 'fellowship with Christ'.[46]

But there is a moving scene in Zeffirelli's film, *Jesus of Nazareth*, which puts the problem in perspective. On Easter Sunday morning, the disciples react scornfully to Mary Magdalene's claim that she has seen the Risen Christ. When she has left, Peter and John admit that they believe her. Andrew demands to know how his brother could be so gullible, whereupon Peter remembers that Jesus had said all along that he would rise on the third day: 'I always believed him,' he admits.

'But Peter, you denied him. You denied him three times,' Andrew retorts angrily.

'Yes, I denied him because I was a coward. We're all cowards. We accused Judas of betraying him but we all betrayed him. We all abandoned him,' Peter replies. 'We ate with him, we lived with him, we knew he was the Christ and still we betrayed him.'[47]

If Peter did make such a claim, he was quite correct. The disciples did betray him. They did deny him. And they deserted him—the one who had poured out his life searching for them, loving them and offering them the spiritual springtime which is summed up in the word 'salvation': wholeness, renewal, healing, cleansing, a right relationship with the living, loving God.

A Project

Judas reminds us that, just as the Spring sunshine reveals weeds as well as flowers, so the presence of Jesus exposes our waywardness as well as the fruit of the Spirit. Ask God to point out to you any weeds in the soil of your life which need dealing with before Easter dawns. And as you reflect on the way Jesus' disciples deserted him, pray for families which are disintegrating—because the children are leaving the nest, because there has been a divorce or a bereavement.

A Prayer

O misery of Judas! From this deliver our souls, O God.[48]

Jesus Recoils From His Vocation

After Judas had left the Upper Room, Jesus and his disciples made their way to the Garden of Gethsemane. Knowing that Judas had gone to betray him, Jesus could have changed the venue. He chose not to. This is further evidence that he was not a victim of circumstances; he gave his life willingly for the world he loved.

Nevertheless, having arrived at this place to which he would often retreat, Jesus' vulnerability surfaces. Most human beings shrink from the prospect of physical pain. Most human beings can tolerate only a limited awareness of man's inhumanity to man and other manifestations of evil. Most Christians shudder at the thought of being abandoned by God. And Jesus was human. In Gethsemane, he visibly shrank from the indescribable physical torture and pain he was about to endure, the coating of the world's sin with which he would soon be encrusted, the separation from his much-loved Father, and that costliest call of all—the call to relinquish the reins of his life. To hand them over. No wonder his whole being protested. No wonder he searched for an escape route:

> *Then he went out of the city and up on to the Mount of Olives . . . with the disciples following him. And when he reached his usual place, he said to them, 'Pray that you may not have to face temptation!' Then he went off by himself, about a stone's throw away, and falling on his knees, prayed in these words—'Father, if You are willing, take this cup away from me—but it is not my will, but Yours, that must be done.' . . . He was in agony and prayed even more intensely so*

that he sweated great drops like blood falling to the ground.'

(Luke 22:39–42,44 JBP)

Although Jesus was human as we are, as we saw when Satan sidled alongside him in the wilderness, he could not be side-tracked from his life's mission which was summed up in his motto: 'Your will, not mine.' Just as he used that motto as a weapon against the Enemy, so now, having given vent to his terror, he returned to that still place before God where he could repeat his resolve to say 'yes' to his Father.

A Project

If you are at a cross-roads today with an important choice to make, ask God to give you the courage to make your decision in the way Jesus did, by seeking God's will in the situation and by asking: 'What is best for the Kingdom?' Think, too, of others today—particularly those who struggle with particular temptations, those facing pain and shrinking from it, those caught up in the world's evils. Hold them to the Christ, who knows what it means to struggle and to win, by saying 'yes'.

A Prayer

Jesus, help me to say 'yes' to you.

The Disciples Sleep

While they were in the Upper Room with Jesus, the remaining eleven disciples would each have echoed that prayer we prayed yesterday.

Yet when they reached the Garden of Gethsemane, although Jesus had pleaded with the three who were closest to him, 'The sorrow in my heart is so great that it almost crushes me. Stay here and keep watch with me', and although he prayed 'with loud cries and tears' (Hebrews 5:7), the disciples fell asleep. They 'could not keep their eyes open.' (Matthew 26:38,43)

Three times Jesus pleaded for their support in prayer. Three times they fell asleep. While the disciples slept, the powers of darkness made their descent on the Garden of Gethsemane. By the time they woke up, Jesus' captors had already arrived.

As the Psalmist predicted, a major part of Jesus' sorrow was to be his aloneness:

> *I looked for sympathy, but there was none*
> *for comforters, but I found none.*

(Psalm 69:20)

When they did wake up, the disciples panicked. Instead of tuning into Jesus' needs and wants, they resorted to brute force. Before he could hand himself over to his enemies, Jesus had to control the skirmish which his own followers had inititated. And while their Master was being arrested, the disciples disappeared. Fear forced them to flee.

Jesus knew that this was the way events would unfold. Even so, he loved his sleepy disciples. He understood that grief made them drowsy and that even now they had not fully understood the warnings he had given them. They did not really realize that he was about to be crucified.

A Project

Think of occasions when you have said an enthusiastic 'yes' to God. Did the enthusiasm wear off? Confess your complacency to God and receive his love and forgiveness afresh. Pray today for Christian leaders who are discouraged, disillusioned or burnt out—tempted to give up. Ask God to give them a Spring-like touch of his love that they may enjoy a renewal of energy and vision. Ask God to show you how you can bring encouragement to your leader.

A Prayer

> O Lord Jesus Christ,
> take as your right,
> receive as my gift,
> all my liberty, my memory, my understanding, my will;
> all that I have,
> all that I am,
> all that I can be.
> All is yours,
> dispose of it according to your will.
> Give me your love.
> Give me your grace.
> It is enough for me.[49]

Jesus Hands Himself Over to His Captors

While Jesus was rousing his disciples for the third time, he could see through the foliage the column of lanterns and flaming torches moving towards him, hear the clank of the metal shields and the murmur of many voices, and he knew that his sword-carrying captors had arrived.

Judas headed the huge, aggressive procession. The traitor had given the crowd a signal: 'The man I kiss is the one you want. Arrest him!' Making a bee-line for Jesus, Judas kissed him and greeted him, 'Peace be with you.' (Matthew 26:48,49)

John reminds us that:

> *Jesus knew everything that was going to happen to him, so he stepped forward and asked them, 'Who is it you are looking for?'*
>
> *'Jesus of Nazareth' they answered.*
>
> *'I am he,' he said . . .*
>
> *When Jesus said to them, 'I am he,' they moved back and fell to the ground.*

(John 18:4,5,6)

The well-armed guard clearly expected Jesus to resist. When he abandoned himself to them with the calm, controlled words, 'I am he', they seem temporarily to have been stunned by his majesty. Or did they glimpse his divinity? We are not told why they fell to the ground. We are told that they seized him and subjected Jesus to the usual brutality: they seized his wrists, twisted his arms, tied his hands behind his back, flung a noose around his neck and led him, like a lamb being taken to the slaughter house, out of the Garden of Gethsemane and into Jerusalem where his mock trial was to take place.

A Project

Re-read the meditation in the project on page 30: 'The Seriousness of Sin'. There I described people as flawed boats which leak oil into the sea of life, polluting every part of God's world. If we introduce Jesus into that picture, we may imagine him like a liner sailing on the polluted, storm-tossed ocean. The fierce waves flood the deck, infiltrate every part of the ship's hold and batter its sides. The liner seems to have abandoned itself to the angry waves and threatens to disintegrate. Yet it does not add to the pollution. It leaks only a detergent, salvation, which counter-acts the activity of the pollution. This week, as we watch the ship sink under the weight of the polluted water, ask God to reveal to you the real situation. You deliberately contributed to the ship-wreck but you were caught up in something much bigger than yourself: a catastrophe of international proportions. You were helpless to help yourself, which was why you needed a Saviour.

A Prayer

> Lord Jesus Christ,
> have mercy on me,
> a sinner.

Peter's Denial

When Jesus emerged from his encounter with Caiaphas, he might well have echoed those words from Lamentations: 'Look around and see. Is any suffering like my suffering?' (Lamentations 1:12). What caused him most pain at that moment? The intrigue? The deceit? His physical wounds? His weariness? His loneliness? His disciple's denial? Or the pain he knew Peter would suffer as he wept out the bitterness of his failure? When Jesus was arrested and taken, first to Annas and then to Caiaphas, Peter followed at a safe distance. Somehow, he managed to gain admission to the courtyard where Jesus had been taken:

> *A fire had been lit in the centre of the courtyard and Peter joined those who were sitting round it. When one of the servant-girls saw him sitting there at the fire, she looked straight at him and said, 'This man too was with Jesus!' But Peter denied it, 'Woman, I don't even know him!' After a little while a man noticed Peter and said, 'You are one of them too!' But Peter answered, 'Man, I am not!' And about an hour later another man insisted strongly, 'There isn't any doubt that this man was with Jesus, because he also is a Galilean!' But Peter answered, 'Man, I don't know what you are talking about!' At once, while he was still speaking, a cock crowed. The Lord turned and looked straight at Peter, and Peter remembered that the Lord had said to him, 'Before the cock crows tonight, you will say three times that you do not know me.' Peter went out and wept bitterly.*

> (Luke 22:55–62 GNB)

We have no way of telling what inflicted most pain on Jesus. We do know, however, that his concern for Peter was deep and real. Peter was one of the first people to whom he appeared after he had risen from the dead (see Luke 24:12 and 34) and eight days later, when Jesus talked privately with Peter on the beach by the Sea of Galilee, just as Peter had denied Jesus three times, so Jesus gave him three opportunities to affirm his love and commitment to the Master.

A Project

Ask God to remind you of occasions when you have disappointed yourself and God. Ask him to apply the ointment of his love to the memory in a way which enables you to enjoy a spiritual springtime. Ask him, too, to recommission you just as he recommissioned Peter; to give you new opportunities for serving him.

A Prayer

> Take my life and let it be
> Consecrated, Lord, to Thee,
> Take my moments and my days,
> Let them flow in ceaseless praise.
>
> Take my love, my Lord, I pour
> At Thy feet its treasure store,
> Take myself and I will be,
> Ever, only, all for Thee.[50]

Judas Commits Suicide

When Jesus was arrested, all his followers fled for their lives. Their desertion seems to have been temporary, because first John and then Peter appear in the courtyard. Judas also seems to have hovered in the background awaiting the verdict of Jesus' trial. Did he expect Jesus' innocence to be recognized? Did he anticipate that Jesus would use his power to confound the religious leaders? We are not told. We are told that the chain of events knocked Judas off balance:

> *Early in the morning, all the chief priests and the elders of the people came to the decision to put Jesus to death. They bound him, led him away and handed him over to Pilate, the governor. When Judas, who had betrayed him, saw that Jesus was condemned, he was seized with remorse and returned the thirty silver coins to the chief priests and the elders. 'I have sinned,' he said, 'for I have betrayed innocent blood.'*
>
> *'What is that to us?' they replied. 'That's your responsibility.'*
>
> *So Judas threw the money into the temple and left. Then he went away and hanged himself.*
>
> (Matthew 27:1–5 NIV)

Judas had heard Jesus tell the story of the Prodigal Son. He had also been present when Jesus had brought wholeness to Zaccheus and publicly forgiven the woman caught committing adultery. He had lived with Jesus for three years. In his head, he knew that he had only to seek forgiveness for the greed and pride which had given rise to his treachery, and it would be granted. But it would appear that the truths he had grasped with his mind had not descended into his heart or affected his will. He remained unchanged by them.

A Project

Think of ways in which Christians today cover Jesus with kisses and pray to him with words of peace on their lips, but betray him with their actions. Pray that they may determine to live differently and seek forgiveness from Jesus himself. Ask God to remind you of occasions when you have betrayed, denied or deserted him. Similarly, ask for forgiveness, and go on to receive it, knowing that he delights to set us free from our past. And pray that the truths which you have grasped with your mind may make the long journey from your mind to your heart, so that you can be changed by them.

A Prayer

> Rock of ages, cleft for me,
> Let me hide myself in Thee;
> Let the water and the blood,
> From Thy riven side which flowed,
> Be of sin the double cure,
> Cleanse me from its guilt and power.[51]

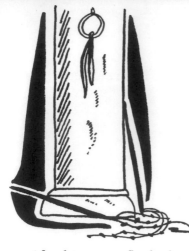

Jesus is Tortured

After his arrest, flanked on each side by heavily-armed Roman soldiers, Jesus was marched to the big, double courtyard near the homes of Annas and Caiaphas, the High Priest. From the time Jesus arrived at the house of Caiaphas to the time he was crucified, he encountered one kind of evil after another. Not one of his friends supported him. This in itself would have been hard to bear. But there was worse to come—including all kinds of violence.

While Jesus was being questioned by Annas, the Romans not only kept their victim bound like a convicted criminal—when they disapproved of the way he responded to the questions Annas was putting to him, the guards slapped him in the face. Some time later, at the end of the trumped-up trial before Caiaphas, the guards 'spat in his face and beat him; and those who slapped him said, "Prophesy for us, Messiah! Guess who hit you!" ' (Matthew 26:67–68)

Things became even more grave. When Pilate sentenced Jesus to death:

> *Pilate's soldiers took Jesus into the governor's palace, and the whole company gathered round him. They stripped off his clothes and put a scarlet robe on him. Then they made a crown out of thorny branches and placed it on his head, and put a stick in his right hand; then they knelt before him and mocked him. 'Long live the King of the Jews,' they said. They spat on him, and took the stick and hit him over the head. When they had finished mocking him, they took the robe off and put his own clothes back on him.*
>
> (Matthew 27:27–31 GNB)

In addition to the torture Jesus endured patiently and silently, he submitted himself to wrongful conviction because of fabricated evidence. Jesus knew and Caiaphas knew that it was illegal for a trial to take place at night. Jesus knew and Caiaphas knew that a man could not be condemned on his own evidence. But Jesus' trial took place at night and he was convicted of 'blasphemy' because he himself admitted to being the Messiah.

> *He who clothes Himself in light as in a garment, stood naked at the judgement; on His cheek He received blows from the hands which He had formed.*[52]

A Project

Ask God to remind you of occasions when you have been wrongly accused or ill-treated. Pray that those memories may be touched and healed. And ask for the grace to forgive those wł o have wronged you. Ask God to remind you of occasions when you have wrongly accused or ill-treated others, and receive his forgiveness.

Pray for all prisoners—particularly those who have been wrongly convicted. Pray especially for Christians in prison who are trying to bring hope to fellow inmates. And pray for victims of violence throughout the world.

A Prayer

Lord, as your Body was broken for me, may I be ready to suffer for you.

The Way of the Cross

Like a sapling he grew up in front of us,
like a root in arid ground.
Without beauty, without majesty (we saw him);
No looks to attract our eyes . . .
And yet ours were the sufferings he bore,
ours the sorrows he carried.
But we, we thought of him as someone punished,
struck by God and brought low.
Yet he was pierced through for our faults,
crushed for our sins.
On him lies a punishment that brings us peace,
and through his wounds we are healed.

(Isaiah 53:2,4,5 JB)

Jesus is Sentenced to Death

Paul once claimed: 'The Son of God . . . loved me and gave himself for me' (Galatians 2:20). Jesus once said, 'Greater love has no man than this, that he lay down his life for his friends' (John 15:13). As we gaze, in our imagination, at the bedraggled figure of Jesus emerging from the public scourging ordered by Pilate, these two verses take on a new meaning.

Jesus had had no rest and no food since he left the Upper Room where he had celebrated the Passover with his disciples. His eyes would almost certainly be bloodshot and puffy, his brow bleeding, maybe men's saliva still clung to his beard, and he would have aged noticeably as Pilate brought him before the crowd and made his now-famous proclamation: 'Behold the man!' (John 19:5). Maybe his mother and his followers, if they had joined the crowd by this time, had difficulty in recognizing him.

Already weakened by all he had suffered, Jesus now faced a further humiliation. As always during the Passover celebrations, Pilate invited the Jews to choose which prisoner he should release. The choice lay between Barabbas, who had been imprisoned for murder and insurrection, and Jesus.

> *'Which one do you want me to release to you?' asked the governor.*
>
> *'Barabbas,' they answered.*
>
> *'What shall I do, then, with Jesus who is called Christ?' Pilate asked.*

They all answered, 'Crucify him!'

(Matthew 27:21,22 NIV)

Pilate continued to plead Jesus' innocence. But the mob clamoured all the more loudly, 'Crucify him! Crucify him!' Whereupon Pilate literally washed his hands of the whole affair—and discovered later that to wash one's hands of God is not as easy as he thought.

A Project

Ask God to remind you of occasions when the Church has washed its hands of its responsibilities. Ask him, too, to remind you of times when you have attempted to wash your hands of things God has asked you to do. Ask for the grace to repent—to think and behave differently. And pray for those who still feel that they can treat God in this cavalier way.

Pray, too, for those who, today, choose evil rather than God. Ask him to remind you of times when you have made cutting remarks to others and thus wounded, even crucified a part of their personality. Recall occasions when you have been hurt by the critical or sarcastic comments which people have made about you and ask God to heal you by showing you how he feels about you.

A Prayer

Lord Jesus Christ, we thank you for all the
benefits you have won for us,
for all the pains and insults you have borne for us.
Most merciful redeemer, friend and brother,
may we know you more clearly,
love you more dearly
and follow you more nearly,
day by day.[53]

Jesus Embraces His Cross

Jesus once said to his disciples: 'I am the good shepherd. The good shepherd gives his life for the sake of his sheep . . . I lay down My life . . . No one is taking it from Me, but I lay it down of My own free will' (John 10:11,17,18, JBP). This is the back-cloth against which the Passion drama is enacted.

After Pilate had washed his hands of Jesus, he handed him over to his captors who evidently loaded Jesus with his cross. As John tells us, Jesus 'went out, carrying his cross' (John 19:17). Down the centuries, artists have painted him positively embracing his Cross—receiving it as the tool he needed to accomplish his mission—the salvation of the world.

Although most artists portray him carrying a complete cross, it was probably only the cross-beam which he was compelled to carry. The upright beam was almost always left at the place of execution. If this assumption is correct, we may picture the battered, bruised, bedraggled, bleeding figure of Jesus, weakened from lack of sleep and want of food and drink, hold out his bound hands to receive the cross-beam—a plank of wood measuring 5in. x 3in. x 6ft. As the beam is loaded onto his right shoulder, it protrudes 30in. in front of him and some 42in. behind, and it perches on the rope which binds Jesus' wrists together. Staggering under the weight of the wood, Jesus is lined up with two convicted criminals and a cohort of Roman soldiers, and as they leave the centre of Jerusalem in convoy, we watch the body of Jesus sway under the weight of the cross-beam as he takes the first steps on this last lap of the journey. Yet the forlorn figure does not plead for pity from us—he is the good shepherd who is giving his life voluntarily for us, his sheep. He yearns for the gratitude which is born of the realization that he is stumbling to Golgotha **for me.**

A Project

As you picture the weary, swaying figure of the cross-carrying Christ, hold to him those who feel they have come to the end of their tether: refugees living in abject poverty, women who have had a miscarriage, any who are angry with God, those locked in conflict with others, those whose marriages seem to be crumbling, the homeless, the suicidal, the unemployed. All who have lost hope. Pray, too, for any who threaten to bring you to the end of your tether, and ask for healing for yourself.

A Prayer

> Suffering Saviour,
> help me to understand
> and feel
> the depth of your love
> for me.
> May it draw from me
> an appropriate response.

Jesus Falls

He before whom all things quake and tremble, to whom every tongue gives praise, Christ the Power of God and the Wisdom of God, is struck on the face by the priests, and they give Him gall to drink. Yet He was pleased to suffer all things, wishing to save us from our sins by His own blood, in His love for mankind.[54]

That is how the Orthodox Church sums up the awesome mystery we are contemplating this week.

As he continued his rescue bid, Jesus continued to travel in convoy with the convicted criminals. Flanked on all sides by spear-carrying Roman soldiers, the condemned wound their way along the narrow, uneven paths of Jerusalem. The sun would have been high in the sky by this time. The heat intense. The pathetic procession could move only slowly, partly because Jesus was too weak to hurry and partly because people would have been lining the streets of this heavily-populated part of the city.

The armed soldiers and the centurion (who headed the procession on horse-back) would have controlled the crowd with their spears, but they could do nothing to control the body of Jesus. It would appear that he lost his balance, lurched forward and fell, unable to steady himself because his hands were still bound by the rope and burdened with the big beam. Neither could they compel Jesus to continue to carry his own cross. Strength had ebbed from him. He was powerless—like someone with a slipped disc whose body seems locked and full of pain. Instead, 'they came across a man from Cyrene . . . and forced him to carry Jesus' cross.' (Matthew 27:32)

The Gospel writers do not actually give details of such a fall, but it would seem probable that this was the reason why Simon of Cyrene was coerced into carrying Christ's cross. The Bible does describe how Jesus was probably feeling at this stage of the journey:

> *My strength has drained away like water,*
> *and all my bones are out of joint.*
> *My heart melts like wax;*
> *my strength has dried up like sun-baked clay;*
> *my tongue sticks to my mouth,*
> *for you have laid me in the dust of death.*

> (Psalm 22:14,15)

A Project

Hold into the arms of the Christ who collapsed under the weight of the cross those who today are feeling that they can't carry on—particularly those who stand by and watch loved ones suffer and die, and all who work in the hospice movement.

Think of occasions when you have felt as though you could not carry on, and ask God to touch and heal the memories.

A Prayer

> O Lord, don't stay away.
> O God, my Strength, hurry to my aid. (Psalm 22:19)

Simon Carries Jesus' Cross

Jerusalem is a beautiful city. But as Simon of Cyrene entered it on that first Good Friday, he was greeted, not by the familiar sights and sounds but by an ugly, unforgettable scene—two convicted criminals carrying crosses, guarded by Roman soldiers whose shields and swords glinted in the sunshine, and the mangled body of a man lying in a state of collapse under the cross-beam of a cross he could no longer carry.

Did Simon stop to stare at the pathetic figure? Is that why he was commandeered into carrying Christ's cross? Or was it because, as Jim Bishop has suggested, his 'brown, bulging biceps'[55] suggested that he could carry the thirty-pound beam with comparative ease? We are not told. We are simply informed that when the Roman soldiers had tired of their sport of scourging and mocking Jesus, they led him away to be crucified and 'Simon of Cyrene, who was coming in from the country just then, was pressed into service to carry Jesus' cross' (Mark 15:21).

When Simon came on the scene, the strange procession wore a different complexion. Jesus' cross was loaded onto the unwilling, resentful Simon while Jesus willingly continued to drag one foot after the other all the way to Golgotha.

We are not told whether Simon and Jesus spoke to one another. Neither are we told whether Simon waited to watch Jesus being stripped and nailed to the cross; whether he was among the crowd who heard him forgive the penitent thief, offer comfort to his mother, abandon himself into the arms of his Father and then die. We are told by Mark that 'Simon is the father of Alexander and Rufus' (Mark 15:21). Many have deduced from this that Simon's sons were well known to the earliest Christians and that, in all probability, Simon lingered at the foot of the Cross and that on Good Friday he was converted to Christianity.

A Project

Simon's story reminds us that being involved with others is risky and costly. It can hurt. That is one reason why we steer clear of the tramp sitting on the park bench or sleeping in the bus shelter, why we shrink from sharing the desperation of people living in squalor in the inner cities and elsewhere, why we would rather dispense charity by writing a cheque than roll up our sleeves and become involved.

Ask God to show you how you can come alongside someone in need and support and strengthen them.

A Prayer

> Lord, for the times I fail to help carry other people's burdens . . .
> for the times I fail to share whatever you have given me . . .
> for the times I do not welcome strangers . . .
>   have mercy.
>
> Lord, heal my lack of openness to others. Help me to make the first move to welcome others.[56]

Constant Concern for Others

Too weak to carry his own cross, a cause of concern for the centurion in charge of the procession, Jesus' reaction to the 'women of Jerusalem' must surely have surprised everyone. In all probability, these women were part of an organized group who were called 'the charitable women of Jerusalem.' They were official mourners, people with permission to offer sedative drinks to condemned criminals. When they saw Jesus dragging one foot after the other along the rough road, they seem to have had genuine pity for him. Their tears seem to have been real tears of sorrow. Yet Jesus summons the strength to say to them:

> *Daughters of Jerusalem, do not weep for me; weep rather for yourselves and for your children. For look, the days are surely coming when people will say, 'Blessed are those who are barren, the wombs that have never borne children, the breasts that have never suckled!' Then they will begin to say to the mountains, 'Fall on us!'; to the hills, 'Cover us!'*

(Luke 23:28–30 JB)

Even the most selfless person, when suffering, finds it hard to think of anything but their own pain. Not so Jesus. Despite his physical frailty, he seems to have ignored his own pain and concerned himself with the anguish these women and their children would suffer when Jerusalem was razed to the ground and those who survived the atrocities were taken into exile.

A Project

Spend some time drinking in Jesus' concern for the women of Jerusalem and their children. Become aware that he is equally concerned today for women and children all over the world. So bring to the surface of your memory mothers who, today, must watch their children die from disease, starvation, injuries inflicted by terrorists or accident. Recall pictures of those you have seen on television or in magazines. Think of mothers whose children are 'lost' because they have run away to the big cities of our country. Think of parents in some Third World countries who have been forced to sell their children as slaves or prostitutes. Hold such people in the presence of the Christ who is always concerned about the plight of the poor.

A Prayer

Lord,
Thousands of children have been herded into refugee camps
where they live separated from their mothers.
Thousands of children have lost their mothers
through war and famine, floods and earthquakes.
Thousands of families climb into boats where they starve
because they cannot find a hospitable port.
The big, brown eyes of these children stare out at me,
I can count their ribs but I don't know how to respond
to wave after wave of such human tragedy.
Show me what I can do.
Then help me to do it.

A Dignified Death

At last the procession reaches its destination: Golgotha, the place which looked like a skull, the place of execution. There they stripped Jesus in the way the Psalmist once foretold:

> *The enemy, this gang of evil men, circles me like a pack of dogs; they have pierced my hands and feet. I can count every bone in my body. See these men of evil gloat and stare; they divide my clothes among themselves by a toss of the dice.*

> (Psalm 22:16–18 LB)

The soldiers did just that: 'The soldiers threw dice to divide up his clothes among themselves. Then they sat around and watched him as he hung there.' (Matthew 27:35,36)

The soldiers were not the only ones to leer. The bystanders, it seems, were equally intent on humiliating Jesus. As he hung, naked, from his cross, they ridiculed him:

> *And the people passing by hurled abuse, shaking their heads at him and saying, 'So! You can destroy the Temple and build it again in three days, can you? Well, then, come on down from the cross if you are the Son of God.'*

> (Matthew 27:39,40)

A Project

If you have ever been to hospital, and been asked to take off your own clothes and sit in a waiting room, or worse, a corridor, wearing an ill-fitting hospital robe which doesn't fasten properly, you will know how humiliating and degrading it can be to be stripped of your clothes. Pause to ponder on the fact that Jesus was further humiliated. When he was nailed to his cross, he was both naked and alive. Yet he did not lose his dignity.

Pray for victims of rape and incest. Pray, too, for prostitutes and strippers, all who abuse the bodies of others, treating them as toys, all who commit sexual offences, the writers of pornographic literature and producers of 'blue movies'.

Think of occasions when you have misused your God-given gift of sexuality, or of occasions when you would have abused this gift if the opportunity had presented itself. Lay your immodest and impure thoughts and jokes at the feet of the naked, crucified Christ, and receive his forgiveness.

Think of occasions when you have been used—either sexually or in some other way—and ask for a healing touch from God.

A Prayer

> You were wounded and bruised for my sins
> You were chastised that I might have peace
> Your flesh was lacerated—
> and I am healed.
> Hallelujah to you, Lord Jesus.

Freely Forgives

Having stripped Jesus of his clothes, they crucified him.
'Let us try to picture the scene,' invites Canon Peter Green.

> *The Cross is laid on the ground. Jesus is stripped and thrown
> roughly onto the Cross. Nails are driven through each hand
> and foot. The Cross is jerked up, throwing the whole weight of
> the body upon the tortured hands and feet. Then with a
> sickening jar the Cross is dropped into the hole prepared for
> it, and wedges of wood are driven in to stay and support it,
> each blow of the hammer sending a thrill of agony through the
> whole of our Lord's Body. And he meets each fresh thrill with
> the often-repeated prayer: 'Father, forgive them, for they know
> not what they do.' For the Greek makes it quite plain that this
> word was not spoken once. The text should be translated 'Jesus
> kept on saying, "Father, forgive them, for they know not what
> they do."'* [57]

That prayer of Jesus, 'Father, forgive them, they don't know what
they are doing' must surely be one of the most moving on record. It also
gives us a glimpse of the victory he was winning on Calvary's tree. For
the Greek word 'to forgive' is *aphesis*. This is the word Jesus used at the
grave of Lazarus when, having called Lazarus from the tomb, he invites
his friends to *aphesis*, 'loose him', set him free from the grave-clothes
which were still wrapped around his face and body. Release him from
the shackles of death.

Here on the cross, Jesus uses the same word. While the soldiers were
in the act of crucifying him, while he was being mocked and ridiculed
and while the events of Judas' betrayal, Peter's denial, the disciples'

desertion were still fresh in his memory, Jesus seems to plead with the Father, 'Abba, loose them, let them go, set them free to become the people you always intended them to be. Release them from the tyranny of self-pleasing. Restore to them their birthright—the one-ness with you for which they were created.'

A Project

If 'to forgive' means to let go, to refuse to forgive means to cling. If to forgive means to take off the restricting grave-clothes, to refuse to forgive means to tie up; to bind. Think of occasions when you have hurt or failed someone and they have forgiven you. Thank God for such times.

Ask him to show you whether there is anyone you are refusing to forgive. Cling to a table or chair for a moment. Notice how you lose your freedom of movement when you cling to something. Be aware that when you refuse to forgive someone you are in bondage to them and they to you. Ask for the grace to let go so that you and the person concerned can enjoy the freedom Christ died to win for you. [58]

A Prayer

Forgive us our sins as we forgive those who sin against us.

At the Foot of the Cross

He was pierced for our transgressions,
he was crushed for our iniquities;
the punishment that brought us peace was upon him,
and by his wounds we are healed.
We all, like sheep, have gone astray,
each of us has turned to his own way;
and the Lord has laid on him
the iniquity of us all.

(Isaiah 53:5–6 NIV)

Warmly Welcomed

Jesus was not crucified alone. Two convicted criminals were killed with him. They would have walked to Calvary in convoy with Jesus. They would have watched him fall, seen how Simon of Cyrene was compelled to carry his Cross, and they would have been aware that Jesus was unlike most men facing crucifixion. As Canon Peter Green reminds us, 'Crucifixion, where the victim died of exhaustion, cramp, thirst, and pain, was said to be the most awful of deaths, and the curses and yells of crucified men were often so appalling that the bystanders could not endure them.'[59]

Jesus, on the other hand, behaved more like 'the most heroic of martyrs'. When he spoke, it was in words like the prayer we meditated on yesterday: 'Father, forgive them . . .' Yet the thieves reacted very differently to Jesus:

> *One of the criminals hanging there hurled insults at him: 'Aren't you the Messiah? Save yourself and us!' The other one, however, rebuked him, saying, 'Don't you fear God? You received the same sentence he did. Ours, however, is only right, because we are getting what we deserve for what we did; but he has done no wrong.' And he said to Jesus, 'Remember me, Jesus, when you come as King!' Jesus said to him, 'I promise you that today you will be in Paradise with me.'*

(Luke 23:39–43)

The penitent thief had read no books about the meaning of Christ's death yet, instinctively, he reached out to Jesus and was accepted.

When he recorded this incident in his Gospel, was Luke trying to assure us that it is never too late to enjoy God's Springtime? Was he also trying to underline that no crime is so serious that it need keep us from experiencing God's love? Whether or not this was the disciple's intention, this story inspired an elderly friend of mine to confess to God that she had lived 'a terrible life'. 'I asked him to forgive me,'she told me. 'And do you know what happened? He set me free from all that filth and evil. Even the guilt has gone. And I don't deserve it after what I've done.'

A Project

Pray for all prisoners. Lift them to the Crucified Christ. Pray,too for others who scarcely dare believe that God will forgive their past. Ask God to remind you of your own failings. Receive his forgiveness.

And re-read the meditations on pages 64–65 and 66–67: 'Jesus Weeps Over Jerusalem' and 'Silent Support', since today is Palm Sunday.

A Prayer

> I may not know, I cannot tell
> What pains you had to bear
> But I believe it was for me
> You hung and suffered there.

The Tender Touch

Just before noon on the first Good Friday, before the light was to go from the sun and darkness was to envelop the world, Jesus became acutely aware of his mother who was standing with 'the beloved disciple' at the foot of the cross:

> *He said to his mother, 'He is your son.'*
>
> *Then he said to the disciple, 'She is your mother.' From that time the disciple took her to live in his home.*
>
> (John 19:25,26)

From the moment Mary had received God's invitation to become the mother of the Messiah, she had said her 'yes' to God and, at great cost to herself, had devoted herself to Jesus. She had not always fully understood his mission (see Luke 2:50 and John 2:4) but she had stayed by him and here she was, loving him to the bitter end.

As the end drew rapidly near, Mary was to need the support of John. The prophet Simeon had warned her that 'sorrow, like a sharp sword, will break your own heart' (Luke 2:35). That surely must have been happening as darkness fell and as she heard her much-loved son complain of thirst, before screaming out to his Father: 'My God, my God, why have you forsaken me?' It must have felt as though someone was turning the sword in her own wound when she watched Jesus slump forward and die before her very eyes. But the memory of that beautiful moment when he noticed her and met her need, despite his own anguish and pain, must have stayed with her forever, and brought some degree of comfort in the desolation of the next day.

A Project

Think of occasions when you have been distraught and God has come to you through the touch or kindness of friends. Thank him—and maybe thank them too.

Pray for those who have no one to draw alongside them when they need help.

Pray especially for children who neglect or deliberately hurt their parents.

Ask God to remind you of occasions when you have not shown your parents the kind of care and concern Jesus showed his mother, and ask for forgiveness.

If you have been hurt by your own children, let go of any bitterness and ask God to heal your inner wounds.

Pray for parents who are struggling to stay alongside their children and to show love, even though they do not understand their offspring's philosophy of life or calling.

A Prayer

Lord,
give me the grace to follow your example.
Create in me the desire and the will
to put the needs of others before my own
even when I am hurting.

The Centurion

What convinced the penitent thief that Jesus was the Messiah? Was it the way Jesus bore his suffering: refusing the pain-deadening draught of cheap wine, expressing forgiveness for his torturers, showing concern for those who could not cope with the sight of his scars? Or was it the majestic silence with which he absorbed the insults and jeers of the soldiers and other bystanders?

We shall never know. We do know that the penitent thief was not the only one to enjoy a touch of God's Springtime on Good Friday. The army officer on duty at the scene of the Crucifixion had a similar experience:

> *At noon the whole country was covered with darkness, which lasted for three hours. At three o'clock Jesus cried out with a loud shout:*
>
> *'Eloi, Eloi, lama sabachthani?' which means, 'My God, my God, why did you abandon me?'*
>
> *Some of the people there heard him and said, 'Listen, he is calling for Elijah!'*
>
> *One of them ran up with a sponge, soaked it in cheap wine, and put it on the end of a stick. Then he held it up to Jesus' lips and said, 'Wait! Let us see if Elijah is coming to bring him down from the cross!' With a loud cry Jesus died . . .*

The army officer who was standing there in front of the cross
saw how Jesus had died. 'This man was really the Son of God!'
he said.

(Mark 15:33–37,39 GNB)

This army officer had been in charge of the soldiers Pilate commanded
to flog Jesus. But this man's heart would have been hardened to such
savage scenes. He would almost certainly have accompanied Jesus as he
staggered from Jerusalem to Golgotha, but the experience was not new.
He had walked that way with the condemned many times before.

When springtime comes to the countryside, the silence of winter is
broken by the tell-tale sound of dripping water as the sun melts snow
and ice. When springtime came to the centurion, his heart-hardness was
melted, scales fell from his eyes and he realized that Jesus was what he
professed to be: God's Son. Such revelations are a sign that the Holy
Spirit is at work. His is the task of showing us the truth about Jesus.

A Project

We are not told what happened to the centurion after the Resurrection.
Some believe that it was he who gave Luke the details he records in his
account of Jesus' death. That suggests that he joined ranks with the
disciples. Try to put yourself in the centurion's sandals. What might you
have done after the Resurrection? What does that tell you about your
commitment to Jesus?

A Prayer

> Spirit of the Living God
> Fall afresh on me
> Break me, melt me, mould me, fill me.

Jesus Dies

We have come to the stage of our journey where we must take only small steps, and stop frequently. We are in the presence of mysteries which reveal their true meaning only to those who will stop to ponder, to worship, to love and adore. The Bible's own words express most powerfully the awesomeness of the death of Jesus:

> *It was now about the sixth hour, and darkness came over the whole land until the ninth hour, for the sun stopped shining. And the curtain of the temple was torn in two. Jesus called out with a loud voice, 'Father, into your hands I commit my spirit.' When he had said this, he breathed his last.*

> (Luke 23:44–46 NIV)

As we observed yesterday, the centurion watching Jesus die praised God and said, 'This man was really the Son of God.' Someone else has expressed the mystery in this way:

> *Today, He who hung the earth upon the waters is hung upon the Cross.*
> *He who is King of the angels is arrayed in a crown of thorns.*
> *He who wraps the heaven in clouds is wrapped in the purple of mockery.*
> *He who . . . set Adam free receives blows upon His face.*
> *The Bridegroom of the Church is transfixed with nails.*[60]

A Project

Take some time today to drink in the fact that Jesus really did die—that he died to save you.

Take some time simply to be quiet before the Cross and adore the Christ who 'loved me and gave himself for me.'

Like the Centurion, make your own response to God's love.

A Prayer

> You are worthy to take the scroll
> and to break its seals,
> because you were sacrificed, and with your blood
> you bought people for God
> of every race, language, people and nation
> and made of them a line of kings and priests for God,
> to rule the world . . .
> Worthy is the Lamb that was sacrificed
> to receive power, riches, wisdom,
> strength, honour, glory and blessing.

(Revelation 5:9,10,12 JB)

> To him who loves us
> and has freed us from our sins by his blood . . .
> be praise and honour, glory and might,
> for ever and ever.[61]

Jesus is Pierced

During the Last Supper, Jesus had taken bread in his hands, blessed it, broken it and offered it to his disciples saying, 'Take, eat, this is my body given for you' and he had taken a cup of wine, blessed it and claimed, 'This is my blood poured out for you' (Luke 22:20). The disciples who had been present at that supper did not realize that they were watching a dramatization of the events they were to witness for real on Good Friday.

Just before he died, Jesus cried out from the cross: 'I am thirsty'.

> *There was a bowl of sour wine standing there. So they soaked a sponge in the wine, put it on a spear, and pushed it up towards his mouth. When Jesus had taken it, he cried, 'It is finished!' His head fell forward, and he breathed his last breath.*

> *As it was the Day of Preparation for the Passover, the Jews wanted to avoid the bodies being left on the crosses over the Sabbath (for that was a particularly important Sabbath), and they requested Pilate to have the men's legs broken and the bodies removed. So the soldiers went and broke the legs of the first man and of the other who was crucified with Jesus. But when they came to him, they saw that he was dead already and they did not break his legs. But one of the soldiers pierced his side with a spear, and at once there was an outrush of blood and water . . . This happened to fulfil the Scripture, 'A bone of him shall not be broken.' And again another Scripture says— 'They shall look on him whom they pierced.'*

> (John 19:29–34,36,37 JBP)

A Project

Re-read the meditations on pages 68–69 and 70–71, 'Jesus Washes His Disciples' Feet' and 'The Last Supper'. And if you possibly can, go to Holy Communion some time today.

A Prayer

Pray this prayer slowly and meditatively

> Jesus,
> may all that is you
> flow into me.
> May your body and blood
> be my food and drink.
> May your passion and death
> be my strength and life.
> Jesus,
> with you by my side
> enough has been given.
> May the shelter I seek
> be the shadow of your cross.
> Let me not run
> from the love which you offer.
> But hold me safe
> from the forces of evil.
> On each of my dyings
> shed your life and your love.
> Keep calling me until the day comes,
> when, with the saints
> I may praise you for ever.[62]

Jesus Dies

A Project

Look back over the meditations of the past three weeks, and reflect on the prayers you have prayed and the resolves you have made.

A Prayer

> When I survey the wondrous cross
> On which the Prince of glory died,
> My richest gain I count but loss,
> And pour contempt on all my pride.
>
> Forbid it, Lord, that I should boast
> Save in the cross of Christ my God;
> All the vain things that charm me most,
> I sacrifice them to His blood.
>
> See from His head, His hands, His feet,
> Sorrow and love flow mingled down;
> Did e'er such love and sorrow meet,
> Or thorns compose so rich a crown?
>
> Were the whole realm of nature mine;
> That were an offering far too small;
> Love so amazing, so divine,
> Demands my soul, my life, my all.[63]

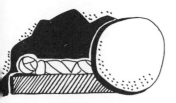

Jesus is Taken Down from His Cross

Jesus has died. His body was broken—for us. His side was pierced and his blood shed—for us.

After the soldier had pierced the side of the Saviour,

> *Joseph of Arimathea, who had been a secret disciple of Jesus for fear of the Jewish leaders, boldly asked Pilate for permission to take Jesus' body down; and Pilate told him to go ahead. So he came and took it away. Nicodemus, the man who had come to Jesus at night, came too, bringing a hundred pounds of embalming ointment made from myrrh and aloes. Together they wrapped Jesus' body in a long linen cloth saturated with the spices, as is the Jewish custom of burial. The place of crucifixion was near a grove of trees, where there was a new tomb, never used before. And so, because of the need for haste before the Sabbath, and because the tomb was close at hand, they laid him there.*
>
> (John 19:38–42 LB)

When Nicodemus first made his secretive, night-time visit to Jesus, he heard the words which now echo round the world: 'God loved the world so much that he gave his one and only Son, so that anyone who believes in him may shall not perish but have eternal life' (John 3:16 LB and NIV).

A Prayer

Lord, I believe.

A Day for Reflection

Today a tomb holds Him who holds the creation in the hollow of His hand; a stone covers Him who covered the heavens with glory.[64]

And, as Jesus' body lay in the tomb, his followers rested:

As the body was taken away, the women from Galilee followed and saw it carried into the tomb. Then they went home and prepared spices and ointments to embalm him; but by the time they were finished it was the Sabbath, so they rested all that day as required by the Jewish law.

(Luke 23:55,56 LB)

Although the women and the disciples appear to have kept the letter of the law and observed the strict rules about travel and work, it seems probable that their minds took little rest that day. Perhaps it was even on this day that the disciples and the women began to put together some of the pieces of the jigsaw which made up the picture of Christ's Passion. As each recalled their memories of Jesus and certain sayings, a more complete picture would begin to emerge.

There is great value, I find, in making Holy Saturday as quiet a day as possible—if possible, going away to be still and to rest with God. It is a day, like Good Friday, for going back over the mysteries we have pondered over the past few weeks. To let them sink into our hearts so that they affect our wills.

A Project

There is value, too, in doing a project which the earliest Christians did on this day: to prepare either to make or to renew our Baptism vows. To decide whether we can answer the penetrating questions put to us as Easter dawns:

Do you turn to Christ?
I turn to Christ.

Do you repent of your sins?
I repent of my sins.

Do you renounce evil?
I renounce evil.

Do you believe and trust in God the Father, who made the world . . .
In his Son Jesus Christ, who redeemed mankind . . .
In his Holy Spirit, who gives life to the people of God?
I believe and trust in him.[65]

A Prayer

Jesus
buried in the tomb,
Jesus in burial bands,
you are life
and the source of life;
you are the seed in the earth,
the secret of the Eternal Spring;
you are the wonder of Heaven
and love's unending flowering.

Grant to us all,
Lord Jesus,
that in the soul's long winters
we may patiently
grow imperceptibly,
in the rhythms and seasons
of your love
and so enter into your peace.[66]

He is Risen

Very early on Easter Day, while it was still dark, Mary Magdalene and some of the other women made their way to the tomb. Presumably they intended to anoint Jesus with the ointment they had made on the evening of Good Friday. John reminds us that none of them yet realized the Scripture which said that Jesus must rise from the dead (see John 20:9). While Mary was alone, wailing at the tomb, she turned from the yawning grave and saw Jesus standing there, 'without knowing that it was Jesus.'

> *'Why are you crying?' Jesus said to her. 'Who are you looking for?' She, supposing that he was the gardener, said, 'Oh, sir, if you have carried him away, please tell me where you have put him and I will take him away.'*
>
> *Jesus said to her, 'Mary!'*
>
> (John 20:16)

And the extent of Mary's joy can only be imagined.
But, as Archbishop Anthony Bloom reminds us:

> *The joy of the Resurrection is something we . . . must learn to experience, but we can experience it only if we first learn the tragedy of the Cross. To rise again we must die. Die to our hampering selfishness, die to our fears, die to everything which makes the world so narrow, so cold, so poor, so cruel. Die so that our souls may live, may rejoice, may discover the spring of life. If we do this then the Resurrection of Christ will have come down to us also . . . the Resurrection which is joy,*

the joy of life recovered, the joy of the life that no-one can take away any more! The joy of a life which is superabundant, which, like a stream runs down the hills, carrying with it heaven itself reflected in its sparkling waters . . . It is not only with our hearts but with the totality of our experience that we know the risen Christ. We can know him day after day as the Apostles knew him. Not the Christ of the flesh . . . but the everliving Christ . . . Christ, once risen, is ever alive, and each of us can know him personally. Unless we know him personally we have not yet learnt what it means to be a Christian. [67]

A Project

We have spent several weeks contemplating Christ's death. Work through the Resurrection appearances in a similar way over the next few weeks. And since an accurate understanding of Christ's Resurrection changes our perspective on everything—including his death, you might then like to come back to this book and work through the meditations again.

A Prayer

> I know that my Redeemer lives,
> and that he shall stand upon the earth at last.
> And I know that after this body has decayed, this body shall see God!
> Yes, I shall see him, not as a stranger, but as a friend!
> What a glorious hope!

(Job 19:25–27 LB)

Group Work

I am aware that Church groups sometimes search for Lent material. I am aware, too, that special Lent groups are often formed. The following suggestions may be adapted for groups of all kinds, as well as by prayer partners or prayer triplets who would like to explore God's springtime together. Some groups will be happy to use the suggestions as they stand, others might like to supplement them with the thoughts, prayers and music which make up the tape *God's Springtime*.

Each week it might be helpful to follow this pattern:

1. Begin by playing a piece of quiet music to help members of the group focus away from the busyness of the day and onto God: the tapes *Open to God*, *Reaching Out* and *Laudate* have been designed with this purpose in mind.

2. Remind members of the group of the overall theme of the week, and choose a Bible passage as the focus.

3. Include time for 'faith sharing'— that is, encourage group members to share their own experience. Such sharing is not for discussion, but rather to enrich each member of the group, so encourage members simply to listen, and to receive as a gift any contribution individuals might choose to make.

4. End with a time of prayer and worship. Some groups will want this to be in silence. Others might like to pray 'bidding' prayers—just mentioning before God a person or situation they are concerned about. Other groups may choose to spend time in spontaneous prayer and praise.

Week 1: Beckoned by Love

1. Play a quiet piece of music, such as 'I gave my life for you' or 'My peace I leave you' from the *Open to God* tape.

2. Read the story of the Prodigal Son from Luke 15.

3. Invite members of the group to describe an occasion when they became aware that they were loved by God. Discourage discussion. Encourage the group to listen so that everyone grows in their awareness that God reveals his love in a variety of ways.

4. Invite the group to close their eyes and recall the good things that have happened for them in the past twenty-four hours. Then encourage them to share, perhaps just with the person sitting next to them, one or two of those good things which are signs of God's loving attentiveness.

5. Reflect on the stories which have been shared. Perhaps, between them, members of the group have discovered that the compassionate God is waiting and watching, loving and coming?

6. Encourage members of the group to tell God they want to enjoy his Springtime.

7. Play the song from the *God's Springtime* tape: 'Come as you are.'

8. Pray the prayer on p.16. Pray for people who, like the prodigal son,

have wandered away from the Father.

Week 2: With Jesus in the Wilderness

1. Play the song 'Come as you are' from *God's Springtime*.

2. Read Luke 4:1–13: Jesus' Temptation in the Wilderness, and the meditation on pages 30–31: 'The Seriousness of Sin'.

3. Think of some of the advertisements which are appearing on hoardings and on television at the moment. Would you say that any in particular are appealing to our love of possessions, popularity or power? Describe them and explain how you feel they affect people.

4. Think of the way Jesus handled temptation. Supposing he was here in human form today, how might he react to the adverts you've referred to?

5. Invite individuals to suggest reasons why Jesus emerged from his encounter with Satan strengthened, whereas many of us are defeated day after day.

6. Play the song: Lord, have mercy from the *God's Springtime* tape.

7. Pray for our world which accepts as normal the things Satan was using to side-track Jesus.

8. Say together the prayer at the end of the meditation on page 37, 'One of Satan's Ploys'.

Week 3: With Jesus on the Mount of Transfiguration

1. Play the song 'Breathe on me' from the *Open to God* tape.

2. Read the account of the Transfiguration from Luke 9:28–36.

3. Read the Thought for This Week from 'More Glimpses of Glory' on page 47.

4. Invite individuals to share memories of occasions when they have sensed and seen God's glory. Encourage the others to listen, rather than discuss.

5. Invite individuals, too, to recall times when they have seen God's glory shining through people, and to tell the group about one such instance.

6. Play the song 'The name of Jesus' from the *God's Springtime* tape. Pray that God's Spirit will bring a touch of spiritual Springtime to each member of the group.

7. Pray for people in pain known to members of the group, that God's glory will shine through their frailty.

Week 4: Journey to Jerusalem

1. Play the song 'I gave my life for you' from the *Open to God* tape.

2. Read the account of the Last Supper from Matthew 26:26. Have a loaf of bread or some bread rolls in the room as a visual aid. Encourage people to look at the bread for several minutes, while someone reads Jesus' claims from John 6:35: 'I am the bread of life . . . He who comes to me will never be hungry; he who believes in me will never be thirsty.'

3. Encourage people to reflect on the way bread is made—starting with the sowing of the grain of wheat. Encourage them to share with the group what they know of the process , so that as complete a picture as possible is built up.

4. Now break the bread, while someone reads Jesus' words: 'This is my

body, given for you.' Pass the loaf around so that everyone can take a piece, hold it, feel its texture, smell it and then eat it.

5. Play the song 'Broken for me' from the *God's Springtime* tape. When the group has had time to reflect, ask them to suggest reasons why Jesus chose this particular farewell present.

6. Pray for those who are undernourished—spiritually, emotionally and physically. Mention some individuals by name.

Week 5: The Disciples Disperse

1. Play the Taize chant 'Stay here and keep watch with me' from the *Laudate* tape.

2. Read John 13:21–30.

3. Invite individuals to share occasions when members of their family have been separated for any reason: illness, divorce, children flying the nest, bereavement, war . . . Let them recall how it felt to be separated from loved ones.

4. Ask the group to suggest reasons why all Jesus' disciples deserted him, just when he needed them most.

5. Ask the group to suggest ways in which Christians today desert Jesus even when, like Peter, they promise God always to be on his side.

6. Play the song 'Lord have mercy' from the *God's Springtime* tape. Pray for people whose families are disintegrating and, in particular, pray for the world's 'lost' children, who escape to the big cities and find they have to live rough.

Week 6: The Way of the Cross

1. If possible, have a cross as a visual focus for this meeting.

2. Play the song 'Were you there when they crucified my Lord?' from the *God's Springtime* tape.

3. Read Mark 15:1–38, inviting the group to listen very carefully while someone reads the passage slowly. Suggest to the group that they listen to see if a particular part of the story makes an impact on them, or if a particular word or phrase or sentence seems to stand out. Encourage them to turn any such words over and over in their minds, and to be ready to share them with the group.

4. Ask the group to share with everyone which part of the story moved them most—or whether one of the recent meditations has been special to them. Discourage discussion. Encourage attentive listening, so that each person feels they can share and be heard. Ask people to tell the others if a particular sentence drew them to itself, and to share what the words were.

5. Look at the last verse you read together just now: the centurion's verdict about Jesus. Invite individuals to share with the group what they feel about the Christ who hangs on the cross.

6. Invite everyone to be still, to gaze at the cross and to listen to the song on the *God's Springtime* tape: 'When I survey.'

7. Pray for people who, this Eastertime, know nothing of Jesus or why he died.

8. Pray for the Holy Week Services which will be held in the churches represented in your group.

9. Finish by listening to the last song on the *God's Springtime* tape—'He's alive.'

Notes

1. Stephen Verney, *The Dance of Love*, London: Fount, 1989.
2. Ed. Clifton Wolters, *The Cloud of Unknowing*, London: Penguin Classics, 1978, p.68.

Introduction
3. Gerard Manley Hopkins, quoted 'May Magnificat', Liverpool: Sisters of Notre Dame.
4. Gerard Manley Hopkins, *Spring*, The Pocket Poets, London: Studio Vista, 1969, p.13.
5. Kenneth Grahame, *The Wind in the Willows*, Deane, 1991, p.9.
6. Ephesians 3:16
7. Gerard Manley Hopkins.

Shrove Tuesday—The Start of the Journey
8. Ulrich Schaffer, *Into Your Light*, Leicester: IVP, 1979, p.29.
9. Pascal.

Ash Wednesday—The Waiting Father
10. Macrina Wiederkehr OSB, A *Tree Full of Angels*, copyright © 1988, reprinted by permission of HarperCollins Publishers, p.13.

Thursday—The Compassionate Father
11. Thomas Merton, *Meditations on Liturgy*, Oxford: Mowbrays, 1965, p.107.
12, 13. Henri J.M. Nouwen, *Compassion*, London: DLT, 1982, p.16 and p.18.
14, 15. Thomas Merton, *Meditations on Liturgy*, p.106 and p.107.
16. A Shalom Prayer, published by the Maranatha Community. Copies are obtainable from Westway, Western Road, Flixton, Manchester M31 3LE.

Friday—The Welcoming Father
17. Stephen Verney, *Into The New Age*, London: Fontana, 1976, p.91.

18. Macrina Wiederkehr OSB, A *Tree Full of Angels*, p.154–155.

Saturday—The Forgiving Father
19. Charles Dickens, *David Copperfield*.
20. Jim Borst MHM, *Coming to God*, Guildford: Eagle, 1992.

Sunday—The Tragedy of Sin
21. Ian Petit OSB, *The God Who Speaks*, London: DLT, 1989, p.37.

Tuesday—The Purpose of Temptation
22. *The Alternative Service Book* 1980, OUP, Mowbrays 1980 p.504.

Wednesday—Jesus' Secret
23. John Ernest Bode, 1816–1874.

Friday—Choices on the Journey
24. John Donne.

Sunday—A Glimpse of Glory
25. Source Unknown.

Monday—More Glimpses of Glory
26. Evelyn Underhill, ed. Grace Adophsen Brame, *The Ways of the Spirit*, New York: Crossroad, 1990, p.197.
27. *The Ways of the Spirit*, p.197
28. Macrina Wiederkehr OSB, A *Tree Full of Angels*, p.xiii.

Tuesday—Full of God's Glory
29. Raoul Plus, quoted A *Tree Full of Angels*, p.21.
30. Thomas Merton, 'The Victory', *Collected Poems*, New York: New Directions, 1946, p.115.
31. Jim Borst MHM, *Coming to God*.

Wednesday—Changed into God's Likeness
32. John Powell, *He Touched Me*, Argus, 1974, p.53–54.

33. Edwin Hatch, 1835–1889.

Thursday—Reflecting God's Glory
34. Malcolm Muggeridge, *Something Beautiful for God*, Collins 1971.
35. Mother Teresa, Adaption of a prayer by Cardinal Newman, quoted in Daphne Rae, *Love Until it Hurts*, Hodder and Stoughton 1981.
36. Source Untraced

Friday—Hints of Grief and Glory
37. Patrick Appleforth.

Saturday—Turn it into Glory
38. William Barclay, quoted Meg Woodson, *Turn It Into Glory*, Bethany House Publishers, 1991, p.219.

Sunday—Joy on the Journey
39. A Shalom Prayer.

Wednesday—Silent Support
40. Margaret Gray, *The Donkey's Tale*, S.U. 1984.

Thursday—Jesus Washes His Disciples' Feet
41. Trans. Mr Mary and Arhimandrite Kallistos Ware, *The Lenten Triodion*, Faber and Faber, p.551.
42. Jean Vanier, *The Broken Body*, DLT, 1988, p.72.

Friday—The Last Supper
43. Ulrich Schaffer, *Into Your Light*, p.53.

Sunday—The Disciples Begin to Disperse
44. *The Lenten Triodion*, p.538.
45. *The Lenten Triodion*, p.525.
46. *The Lenten Triodion*, p.538.
47. From the film *Jesus of Nazareth*.
48. *The Lenten Triodion*, p.538.

Tuesday—The Disciples Sleep
49. From the *Spiritual Exercises* of St Ignatius Loyola.

Thursday—Peter's Denial
50. Frances Ridley Havergal (1836–79).

Friday—Judas Commits Suicide
51. Augustus Montague Toplady (1740–78)

Saturday—Jesus is Tortured
52. *The Lenten Triodion*, p.582.

Sunday—Jesus is Sentenced to Death
53. St Richard of Chichester.

Tuesday—Jesus Falls
54. *The Lenten Triodion*, p.586.

Wednesday—Simon Carries Jesus' Cross
55. Jim Bishop, *The Day Christ Died*, Collins 1957, p.289.
56. Peter Cullen, *The Stations of the Cross*, Mayhew McCrimmon, 1981.

Saturday—Freely Forgives
57. Peter Green, *Watchers by the Cross*, Longmans, Green and Co. Ltd., p.15
58. Stephen Verney, *The Dance of Love*, Fount, 1989, chapter 3.

Palm Sunday—Warmly Welcomed
59. Peter Green, *Watchers by the Cross*.

Wednesday—Jesus Dies
60. *The Lenten Triodion*, p.587.
61. *Lent, Holy Week and Easter, Services and Prayers*, SPCK, 1986, p.211.

Maundy Thursday—Jesus is Pierced
62. From the *Spiritual Exercises* of St Ignatius.
63. Isaac Watts (1674–1748).

Holy Saturday—Day for Reflection
64. *The Lenten Triodion*, p.652.
65. Baptismal Promises.
66. Caryll Houselander, *The Stations of the Cross*, Sheed and Ward, p.143.
67. Anthony Bloom, *Meditations on a Theme*, Mowbrays, 1971.